MANAGING
OTHER PEOPLE'S
MONEY

2nd edition

Penny Letts

BOOKS

© 1998 Penny Letts

Published by Age Concern England
1268 London Road
London SW16 4ER

First published 1990
This edition 1998

Editor   Gillian Clarke
Design and typesetting   GreenGate Publishing Services
Production   Vinnette Marshall

Printed in Great Britain by Bell & Bain Limited, Glasgow

A catalogue record for this book is available from the British Library

ISBN 0–86242–250–7

Contents

Foreword

Managing your own money is one thing. Managing other people's money is another.

Within reason you can do what you like with your own money. You can be parsimonious, prudent or prodigal. It's entirely up to you. You don't have to account to anyone else for your actions.

When you are managing other people's money you should have some sort of authority to act. You should act reasonably. You should act in the other person's best interests. And you should be able, if asked, to show how much you have received and how you have spent or invested it.

There are several kinds of authority. Each has its own particular responsibilities. Some, like receivership, have protective mechanisms designed to safeguard the assets being managed. Others, like attorneyship and appointeeship, offer a more user-friendly way of managing other people's money but, conversely, they are also more abuser-friendly.

Penny Letts' book *Managing Other People's Money* is an overview of the different types of authority and the responsibilities that each entails. It provides some good, commonsense ideas on how to use someone else's money to their best advantage, and a number of practical solutions on how to put their affairs in order. Last, but not least, it tells you where to go for help.

Although the book is intended to guide family members through the various perils and pitfalls they may encounter from time to time, I know from my former experience in private practice that it is also an extremely useful addition to any professional adviser's library.

Denzil Lush
Master of the Court of Protection

February 1998

Foreword to the First Edition

With the ageing of the population, many more people who are caring for older relatives or friends need information about managing the financial side of life. There is a great deal of anxiety to do the right things in the right way, but many problems are not serious enough to justify consulting a solicitor or another professional person – or are they? The guidance in this book will be invaluable.

Age Concern deserves everyone's gratitude for its useful publications and I am sure that this will turn out to be one of the most successful. Penny Letts has covered all the main aspects of financial management, for oneself or others, in a straightforward and clear way, free of legal jargon but giving warning of possible traps. The examples illuminate the text and many readers will recognise situations all too familiar to them.

I suspect that one of the sections of the book most often referred to will be the one explaining how to help people with their finances when they don't want to be helped. There are terrible problems involved in that situation. Very often, people postpone making arrangements important for the future, like opening a joint account, making an enduring power of attorney or making a Will; and it's not surprising that the decisions are sometimes put off for so long that it becomes too late, although the person concerned may not accept or understand his or her own incapacity. Following the sensible advice to be found here will give confidence and reassurance.

For some people, the loss of their ability to cope with their finances comes suddenly; for others, as I have said, it is a gradual process. I am conscious that there must be a great deal of informal management going on (often with the best of motives). This book will help to make that management more professional and will indicate when more formal steps should be taken; it should make life easier for the manager and safer for everyone concerned.

Finally, for those of you who are resolute enough to be facing up to your own future, this is the place to learn what you need to know.

A B Macfarlane
Master of the Court of Protection

July 1990

About the Author

Penny Letts is Secretary to the Law Society's Mental Health and Disability Committee, which is concerned with legal issues affecting older people and people with any form of mental or physical disability or disorder. Her work includes the promotion of accessible and comprehensive legal advice and representation for these groups of people, while also trying to achieve improvements in all areas of the law that affect them. She writes regularly on legal issues affecting older people and people with disabilities, and is also a member of the Mental Health Act Commission.

Before joining the Law Society, Penny worked in voluntary organisations providing advice services and working for changes in the law, including the National Council for One Parent Families and the Children's Legal Centre. She is a qualified social worker and has previously worked in local authority social services departments.

Acknowledgements

I thank a number of people who have given me a great deal of help and encouragement in preparing for the first and the second editions of this book.

All members of the Law Society's Mental Health and Disability Committee, both past and present, have allowed me to make use of their knowledge and expertise, but particular thanks are due to Gordon Ashton, Denzil Lush and Lydia Sinclair and to Evelyn McEwen of Age Concern England.

Of the many people who have helped me with constructive comments, encouragement and support, I thank John Seargeant, Alison Matthews, Biddy Macfarlane, Niall Baker and Ashmita Shah. Thanks are also due to the staff of Age Concern England, both those who commented on the draft and those who brought the publication to fruition.

Penny Letts

February 1998

Introduction

One of the basic principles that most of us take for granted is the right to self-determination and individuality. We fiercely protect, so far as possible, the right to make our own decisions about our own lives, including the right to make 'wrong' or unwise decisions. We also try to keep our independence for as long as possible.

In particular, we insist on the freedom to do what we want with our own money and we expect privacy in dealing with our own financial affairs. Obviously the law imposes some restrictions – we have to pay taxes, whether we like it or not, and charges and fees for goods and services. In general, within the confines of the law, people over the age of 18 years have the right to manage their own financial affairs. Some do it badly and run up huge debts; others don't have much to manage. But we all like to decide what to spend our money on, whether to save or invest it, whom we give it to, whom we spend it on – and we have to face the consequences of those decisions.

But there may come a time when we can no longer remain independent, when it is no longer possible to manage alone. We may then need help looking after our financial affairs, on either a temporary or a permanent basis.

People who are ill or physically disabled may need someone else to collect their pension or benefit or go to the bank for them. People who find they are becoming forgetful or confused may wish to ask a person of their choice to attend to matters on their behalf. Others may, through mental frailty, no longer understand what they are doing or be unable to make alternative arrangements for themselves.

This book explains what can be done to take over the management of other people's money and financial affairs. It is written mainly for the people who find themselves in this position – the relatives, carers and friends of those who are no longer able to cope on their own. But it will also be useful for people who want to prepare for a time when, through physical or mental frailty, they may no longer be able to handle their own affairs.

Part 1 presents some situations in which it may become necessary to take over managing other people's money or property, and pinpoints the events that may trigger the need for help. This is done by looking at case examples, showing first some in which help is requested, and, secondly, occasions when it may be necessary to take control of people's financial affairs without their consent, and perhaps even against their wishes.

Part 2 looks at the details of what can be done and how to do it, setting out the powers available, both informal arrangements and statutory powers enshrined in the law. Step-by-step guidance is provided as to what people can do to delegate the management of their affairs and what can and has to be done once you or someone else has to take over.

Part 3 explains the various matters that you may have to deal with in managing other people's financial affairs. First of all money matters – claiming and collecting income, looking after savings and investments, paying the bills, dealing with debts and organising day-to-day expenditure. Next, living arrangements – looking after the upkeep of a property, buying or selling a house, organising a move (eg into residential care). Finally, arrangements to make in helping people to prepare for death – such as making a Will to ensure that family and dependants are taken care of, and dealing with the funeral and other arrangements after death.

Part 4 gives general hints and points to note in the management of other people's money. These stress the importance of keeping careful records and accounts, and suggest other safeguards worth adopting to prevent something going wrong. It also indicates some possible remedies if things do go wrong, and how you can take up complaints.

At the end of the book there is information about where you can obtain further help and advice, with the addresses of relevant organisations and a list of useful publications.

Before using this book

It cannot be stressed too strongly that the management of financial affairs can be extremely complicated and that extra care must be taken when looking after someone else's money or property. In a book of this nature it is possible to give only general advice and guidance. Much will depend on the individual circumstances of the people concerned. It is therefore important to *seek expert help and advice*, in all cases, from sorting out entitlement to state pensions or benefits to managing a valuable and complex estate.

It is also important to recognise that situations may arise in which there is a conflict between your own interests and those of the person whose affairs you are managing. Again, you must seek independent advice.

This book covers only the law in England and Wales. There are major differences in the law in Scotland and in Northern Ireland. Please contact Age Concern Scotland and Age Concern Northern Ireland for details (addresses on p 153).

When to Take Over

Part 1 presents some situations in which it may be necessary or desirable to take over the management of someone else's money. Looking at these examples might help you, as a relative, friend or carer, to identify the point at which your help may be required. It may also help other people to recognise that any of these situations could happen to them, and that it is always wise to make preparations for a time when they may no longer be able to cope for themselves.

Taking control over another person's money or property is a serious matter that should not be done lightly. It is important that control is never taken away from people against their wishes if they are still able to manage for themselves.

Some people may want to delegate some of their affairs to another person, but many people will want to carry on being independent for as long as they can. Perhaps they don't like to ask for help, or they don't want other people meddling in their private affairs. Maybe they think they don't need any help. It is important to do only what is asked of you, or what is necessary.

There will often be particular events or circumstances that will trigger the need for help, such as a sudden illness that means a stay in bed or going into hospital, or a decision to move in with relatives or into residential care. But at other times there will be no clear signal, and action will need to be taken to sort out the affairs of people who are not mentally or physically capable of doing it themselves.

The comments that follow the case studies make suggestions about what sort of help might be needed. Please remember that these are only illustrative and should not be taken as the solution to the problem. Part 2 examines the various solutions available.

Situations That Can Arise

When help is requested

The circumstances in which you may be asked to look after someone else's money or property will usually be fairly obvious. Examples of some typical situations include:

- a bout of sickness or an accident that means staying in bed or being unable to get out of the house;
- going into hospital;
- a physical disability that restricts mobility;
- loss of a partner or other person who has previously helped;
- a change in living arrangements (eg moving in with relatives or into residential care);
- help with a legal transaction (eg the purchase or sale of a property);
- recognition of no longer being able to manage;
- a desire to make preparations for the future.

In all of these situations, the people concerned are likely to know what sort of help they need, how much and how long for. In more complicated cases, there may be a need for independent advice to work out exactly what should be done. The following stories illustrate some of these situations.

> **Freda Mason** was on her way to the post office to collect her pension when she tripped over the uneven pavement. Her neighbour saw the accident and was soon on the scene to help Freda back home and call the doctor. Fortunately, the doctor said that nothing was broken, but it might be a few days before she could walk on her sprained and badly bruised ankle. Freda was worried because she had no shopping in, and no money to pay for it until she could collect her pension.

For Freda help is close at hand. Her neighbour is willing to act as agent (see p 13) to collect her pension for her and to use some of the money to get in the shopping she needs. Freda is likely to be laid up for only a few days, so there is no need for anything else to be done, as she will soon be able to manage for herself again.

Marjorie Evans' accident was more serious. She tripped over a rug in her own home and fractured her femur. She ended up in hospital with her leg in traction and the doctors said it would take a while to heal – at least a couple of months. As a result, she made a list of all the things she needed to ask her daughter to sort out – collecting her pension, paying the rent and other bills. She also needed some money out of the bank for a new nightdress and dressing gown to use while she was in hospital.

Like Freda, Marjorie needed help for only a temporary period, but there were more things to sort out and she was away from home and out of action for a longer time. Luckily, she could deal with most of these matters by making some informal arrangements. She was able to arrange a bank mandate (see p 10) so that her daughter could withdraw money from her account, and she could appoint her daughter as her agent to collect her pension and then pay her bills.

Although Marjorie's leg mended, she still felt unsteady on her feet. On returning home, she found she couldn't manage the stairs very easily and felt nervous about living on her own in case she had another fall. She had been thinking for some time about moving into a residential home and so asked for an assessment of her needs by social services. It was agreed that she needed residential care and arrangements were made for her to move into a private home where her friend already lived. As she isn't very mobile she still needs someone to collect her pension and sort out other matters for her.

It has been suggested to Marjorie that she arranges for the manager of the home to collect her pension along with the pensions of some of the other residents. But that would mean giving up control of her pension book, and she would rather her daughter continued to act for her. Marjorie must also think about what else she would like her daughter to do – such as selling her house. This may mean making a power of attorney (see p 18) to appoint her daughter to deal with the sale on her behalf.

> **Rajesh Patel** suffers from severe arthritis and can't get about very much. He has been managing on his own with the support of his neighbours and the 'home help', and his son calls in as often as he can. Rajesh's son and his wife are considering moving to a larger house with more space for their growing family. They have suggested that Rajesh should sell his house and combine his capital with theirs, so that they can afford a bigger place. They can then offer him a home with them and give him the care he needs. Rajesh likes the idea, but isn't sure he can cope with all the trouble of selling his house and sorting out his finances.

Rajesh could give his son a power of attorney to sort everything out on his behalf. However, this might not be very wise because his son is very closely involved in the arrangements and Rajesh has to make sure that his own interests are protected. Equally, although he gets on very well with his son and daughter-in-law, this might change once they are living together. It is essential that a clear agreement is set out at the start which spells out what would happen if the arrangement broke down. It is very important for Rajesh to get independent legal advice, and it would be as well for him to make sure his other children know what is going on. If Rajesh wishes to make a power of attorney, it would be best to appoint someone who is not involved in the deal, such as a solicitor or someone outside the family.

> **Edward Ford** enjoyed a few years' retirement with his wife before she died last year. He used to be a director of the family business and still takes an active interest, even though his two sons have now taken over the running of it. Edward has a substantial minority share-holding in the company and his sons would like to buy him out. He also has other assets apart from the house where he lives, including building society deposits, long-term gilts and a portfolio of equity holdings. Edward enjoys speculating on the Stock Exchange, but is beginning to realise that his memory is not as good as it used to be nor his judgement as sound.

Edward has a good idea how he wants to use his assets and how he would like to provide for his family. He also has two daughters and he wants them to have a share of the family fortune. He needs to make a Will if he has not already done so. To ensure that his considerable assets are dealt with in the way he wishes, he could also consider making an enduring power of attorney (see p 25), setting out what he wants to happen and whom he wants to manage his affairs when he is no longer able to do so. It would be advisable for Edward to discuss this with the whole family, explaining whom he has chosen to act as his attorney(s) and why, to prevent problems or conflicts between them at a later stage.

When help is not requested

It is likely to be controversial when control over money or property is taken away from people without their understanding or consent or even against their wishes. In these circumstances, some sort of proof may be required, usually in the form of a medical report or opinion, as to the extent to which the person concerned still has the mental capacity to deal with his or her own affairs.

Some examples of particular circumstances in which you may have to take over without consent are:

- to provide for people with a severe learning disability;
- to help people suffering from dementia or other degenerative brain disorders;
- to help people with severe forms of mental illness;
- to help people with brain damage as a result of accident or injury;
- to help people during a period of unconsciousness;
- to deal with arrangements after someone has died without making a Will.

There is currently no universally accepted definition of 'mental incapacity'. It cannot be said that in all situations there are 'right' and 'wrong' decisions to be made, and that someone who reaches the wrong decision is mentally incapable. Nor is it possible to designate certain groups or categories of people, such as those with dementia or learning disabilities, as 'mentally incapacitated', as there will always be varying degrees of understanding and competence within the same group. Even for people with diagnosed mental health problems, their mental capacity may fluctuate over a period of time, and there is no category that can be regarded as corresponding totally with actual incapacity, except perhaps people who are unconscious.

In some cases, the people concerned may have merely lost the ability to communicate, for example following a stroke, but may still be capable of making their own decisions. You should make every effort to find out their views and wishes, by whatever means possible, so that these can be taken into account and, if appropriate, carried out.

In trying to identify when people are no longer mentally capable of managing their own affairs, you should assume that they are capable until they demonstrate otherwise. You must focus on their actual ability to understand and to function in making *particular* decisions: for example, can they go shopping? can they pay their bills? do they know what income they have? If in doubt, always ask for an opinion from the family doctor.

The following case studies may help you to recognise situations in which you might have to take action, even when your help has not been requested or possibly positively refused.

Margaret Wilson hates having to take medication. She has been diagnosed as schizophrenic and knows that taking medication regularly generally keeps her stable. But the drugs cause unpleasant side effects and sometimes she tries to go without, which can result in her becoming very ill. She can rarely remember what happens during these times, and on occasions she has built up debts, which have taken a lot of sorting out. Now that her family know what to expect, they can usually take action before things get in too much of a mess.

In Margaret's case it is important to note that her incapacity to deal with her affairs is temporary, so the arrangements made while she is ill would not need to continue when she has recovered enough to take control of her own affairs again. For example, if Margaret was not working, the family could arrange for the Benefits Agency to pay her Social Security benefits to an appointee (see p 33), probably a relative or friend, who could then use it to pay her rent and bills. If Margaret has a bank account, arrangements could be made for some bills to be paid directly, by direct debit, standing order or monthly payments under a budget payment scheme (see pp 78–79).

> **Mary Barker** collects her pension each week and puts it away carefully. But when she comes to do her shopping, she can never find it and is convinced she must have been burgled. This happens almost every week and the police now refuse to come round any more. Each time, her son searches the flat. Sometimes he finds the money hidden under the carpet or the mattress, or in the tea caddy; sometimes he can't find it at all and has to give Mary some money to tide her over.

So long as Mary's son is willing to help his mother out and tries to make sure she gets her shopping and pays the rent etc before she forgets where the money is, nothing else may need to be done at present. However, if Mary becomes more confused, her son could ask the Benefits Agency to make him Mary's appointee so that he can claim the pension on her behalf, and arrange for her rent and bills to be paid direct.

> **William Ferguson**'s change in behaviour has alarmed his wife Janet – he has been diagnosed as having Alzheimer's disease. William has always looked after the family's financial affairs and has never told Janet much about them. Although they have bank and building society accounts in joint names, Janet knows he has considerable assets in his own name that no one else has any access to, and William refuses to tell Janet anything about them.

William may be well enough to make an enduring power of attorney so long as he is able to understand what he is doing, but if he is refusing help this will not be possible. If he is too ill to make any arrangements himself, there is no alternative for Janet but to apply to the Court of Protection for a receiver (see p 41) to be appointed to deal with his affairs. The Court will need to see a medical report to confirm that William has a mental disorder and no longer has the mental capacity to manage his own affairs.

John Carter was riding his bike home from the library when he was hit by a car. He was unconscious for several days and when he came round he couldn't recognise his wife or son. The doctor has said he suffered severe brain damage and will never fully recover.

An emergency application (see p 47) may have to be made to the Court of Protection to make urgent provision for John's dependants. His wife should also seek advice from a solicitor, as it may be possible to claim an award of damages, which will be needed to pay for John's future care. Advice may also be needed about entitlement to state benefits. The Court of Protection will need to be involved to ensure that any damages are properly invested and managed.

The Powers Available

Part 2 sets out the powers that are available to enable you to take over the management of other people's money or property, beginning with the most informal and ending with those requiring the greatest degree of intervention.

The first two sections describe the arrangements that people can choose to make for themselves, if they are having problems managing on their own, and would like to ask someone else to help, or if they want to prepare for a time when they may no longer be able to cope.

The last two sections look at the powers available to you for taking control of other people's financial affairs when they are no longer capable of making their own arrangements. In these circumstances, you may have to act without their consent or even against their wishes. You will need to follow the correct procedures to ensure that you are not acting without proper authority and that you do not take away their rights unnecessarily.

Informal Arrangements

There are several arrangements that can be made by people, while still mentally competent, who would like someone else to act on their behalf in handling financial matters. This section describes those that can be made informally, without the need for any sort of 'official' approval. People can arrange for you to help them with their financial affairs by:

- authorising you to use their bank or building society account by mandate;
- putting money into a joint account with you;
- appointing you as their agent (eg to collect Social Security benefits or pensions).

Access to bank and building society accounts

People who are physically unable to visit the bank or building society may need someone else to withdraw money or carry out some other transaction on their behalf. It is possible for them to draw up a mandate authorising another person to use their account and undertake such transactions. This is known as a 'third party' mandate, as it enables you (the third party) to take part in arrangements made between the bank or building society and the account holder.

Individual banks and building societies have different requirements for drawing up a third party mandate, and account holders will need to contact their own branch to find out their particular procedures. In some cases a letter of authority from the account holder confirming that he or she wishes you (or another named person) to be a signatory to the account (allowed to use the account on his or her behalf) is sufficient. Some banks and building societies provide forms for completion and signature by the account holder, to be used as proof of authorisation as and when you need it, until it is cancelled. Others require a fresh form to be completed before each transaction.

A third party mandate is revoked if the account holder becomes mentally incapable of managing the account.

Putting money in joint names

Many people living with their spouse or partner will already have joint bank or other savings accounts to pay for joint expenses such as household bills. For people who are finding it difficult to manage their own affairs, there may be advantages in putting some of their funds into joint names, so long as the other account holder is a close and trusted relative or friend.

The *advantages* of a joint account are:

- another person can have easy access to the funds held in the account;
- it may mean lower bank charges;
- if one person dies, any balance on the account passes to and can be used by the other account holder(s) immediately.

The *disadvantages* of a joint account are:

- less financial and personal independence between account holders;
- the possibility of disagreement between account holders;
- if one account holder becomes mentally incapacitated, the account may be frozen until new arrangements can be made.

There is no set limit as to how many people can share an account, so long as the bank or building society agrees. Arrangements can be made for any or all of the account holders to use the account. The joint holders have to sign a mandate stating which, and how many, of them can sign cheques or carry out other transactions. It is also possible for the mandate to say that the account can be used only while it is in credit, thus preventing its becoming unintentionally overdrawn. The mandate can be cancelled at any time by any of the account holders, unless there is an agreement to the contrary. However, the mandate becomes ineffective if one of the account holders becomes mentally incapable of managing the account

Whom will the bank deal with?

The bank must deal with all the account holders. Statements must be sent to all account holders individually unless all those with the joint account have signed an agreement that they wish to receive only one statement between them. This may help to reduce bank charges.

Who is liable for the joint account?

Holders of a joint account are *all* responsible, both jointly and individually, for the account and for the repayment of any debt if the account becomes overdrawn – they are what is called 'jointly and severally liable', unless the mandate agreed by all the account holders states otherwise.

Joint holders are not automatically allowed to use each other's credit. The bank should not lend money to one holder, either by overdraft or by personal loan in joint names, without obtaining from each account holder an undertaking accepting liability for the debt, both jointly and individually. If an overdraft has not been pre-arranged, all the account holders should be kept fully aware of the extent of the borrowing.

Joint holders should be aware that a bank can transfer money from an individual account held by one of the account holders to cover a debt on a jointly held account. This is because the holders of the joint account are jointly and severally liable for any debts. The bank will usually ask permission, but it is possible for them to do this automatically. If the debt is on an individual's account, money from a joint account cannot be transferred to it unless all holders of the joint account agree to this.

If the joint account has a mandate that covers the account only when it is in credit, the holder who signed a cheque that caused the account to become overdrawn would be liable for the debt.

Who owns the money in a joint account?

If all the joint holders pay money into the account, it is presumed that they own the amount held in the account in proportions according to the amounts contributed. In some cases it may be difficult to calculate the exact proportions. If any of the holders does not pay into the account, he or she does not automatically own a share of the money.

However, if the account is held jointly by a husband and wife, the law presumes that the money in the account belongs equally to them both, regardless of who contributes to the account. For joint account holders who are not married, the person who contributes to the account will normally be presumed to own the money, unless it can be shown that it was the clear intention in setting up the joint account that the money would be owned jointly and shared equally or in specified proportions.

Because of the uncertainty that can arise as to who actually owns the money in a joint account held by people who are not married, it is advisable to have a written agreement signed by each of the account holders, confirming their intentions, and to lodge a copy with the bank.

What happens if joint account holders disagree?

If it has been agreed that the holders of a joint account can act alone and then a disagreement arises between them, any one of them could still spend money from the account and could even take all the money. The bank can refuse payment only if the mandate is cancelled by one of the account holders, in which case the account is frozen.

It is therefore essential to cancel the mandate as soon as disagreement occurs. All the holders would then have to negotiate how the money in the frozen account could be used. If they fail to agree, the courts will have to decide how the money should be divided.

What happens if one account holder becomes incapacitated?

If one account holder becomes mentally incapable of managing his or her financial affairs, the mandate for the joint account is terminated automatically, and the bank or building society is entitled to decline any further transactions until it receives fresh instructions from all account holders, including the legally authorised representative of the person who 'lacks capacity'. This may be an attorney appointed under an enduring power of attorney once it has been registered (see p 27), or someone authorised by the Court of Protection or the Public Trustee (see pp 41–55).

Collecting Social Security benefits as an agent

'Agency' is the general name given to the relationship when one person authorises another (the agent) to act on his or her behalf and the agent agrees to do so. Most of us use an agent at some point in our lives, usually for specific purposes; for example, we might use a travel agent to arrange our holiday, or an estate agent to sell our house. Likewise, many people use an agent to handle their financial affairs when they are unable to do so for themselves.

Anyone who collects a Social Security benefit or pension from the post office on someone else's behalf is acting as an agent. It is an arrangement that thousands of older people make with a relative, neighbour, friend or 'home help' to enable their pensions to be collected.

When a person who receives a Social Security benefit or pension, known as the claimant, nominates you as agent, it is a purely personal agreement between you and the claimant, but is accepted by the Benefits Agency and the post office. As agent, you are authorised to collect the money and hand it over to the claimant, but not to spend it or keep it without being told to do so by the claimant.

Who chooses the agent?

The choice of the agent should be left to the claimant, and it is important that he or she is someone the claimant can trust. It is possible for claimants to change their choice of agent at any time.

How to nominate an agent

Where this is a temporary arrangement, the person entitled to the benefit deletes the sentence 'I acknowledge receipt of the above sum', which is printed on the front of the pension or allowance order slip, signs and dates it as usual and completes and signs the declaration on the back of the slip, which says:

'I am the person whose name is on the front of this order book. I am entitled to the amount printed on this order. I authorise [*your name*] to be my agent and to cash this order for me.'

You also have to sign and date the following statement, which is printed on the back of the payment slip:

'I am the agent of the person whose name is on the front of this book, and who is alive today. I have received the amount printed on this order. I will pay this amount to the person whose name is on the front of this order straight away.'

If you have to collect the money on only a few occasions, you and the claimant must sign the above statements each time. If you are likely to be needed for a long time, the claimant can ask the Benefits Agency office to issue you with a card (called an agency card), by completing an application form (Form BF 73) in front of a witness. This card states that you, the agent, are authorised to collect money for the payee (the claimant), and it can be used as identification each time you go to the post office. However, the claimant must still sign each order due for payment, but need only sign on the front.

The Benefits Agency is currently developing plans for paying pensions or benefits by use of a plastic benefit payment card, similar to a credit card. It is not yet clear what arrangements will be made for agents to use these cards, so you may have to ask at the local Benefits Agency office.

Who is responsible for the claim?

The person entitled to the benefit remains responsible for all matters relating to the claim, in particular notifying the Benefits Agency of any relevant change of circumstances. As the agent, you are not responsible for this, but if you notice any changes that should be reported and which may affect the claimant's benefit (eg reaching retirement age), it might be helpful if you pointed these out to the claimant, as it may be necessary to get advice about this.

If the claimant is temporarily too ill to appoint an agent

You may be looking after someone who is temporarily too ill to be able to go through all the procedures to appoint you as an agent. In this case, rather than getting the claimant to sign the slip in the order book, contact the Benefits Agency and explain that the claimant is not well enough to make arrangements to collect his or her benefit. The Benefits Agency can then appoint you to collect and, if necessary, spend the money for the claimant, without any special permission from the claimant. However, you may be asked to provide receipts to show that you have spent the money for the claimant's benefit.

If the claimant is not capable of appointing an agent

Claimants who are not able to understand what they are doing cannot make a valid appointment of an agent. Therefore this method cannot be used to collect benefits or pensions once claimants become too confused to manage their own affairs.

If you are acting as an agent for a claimant who later becomes too confused to understand the arrangement, you should immediately cease to act, and should inform the Benefits Agency that alternative arrangements must be made. It is possible that the Benefits Agency will make you an appointee (see p 33) unless the claimant has previously made an enduring power of attorney (p 25) or some other arrangement.

If the claimant is in residential accommodation

Many claimants in residential accommodation will want to retain control of their finances and make their own arrangements for the collection of benefits or pensions if they are unable to collect these themselves. This will normally be done by appointing a relative or friend as their agent, as described above.

It is sometimes suggested to people who go into residential homes that they should appoint the manager or proprietor of the home as their agent. This is not recommended unless there is absolutely no one else who can act for them. It is important that any staff of residential homes who act as agents for residents keep detailed and careful records of benefits collected and payments made to each individual claimant. The local social services authority should also be notified that such arrangements have been made.

Claimants who are living in a local authority residential home can use what is known as 'alternative agency'. They can nominate an official of the local authority (by office, not by name, and usually a senior officer such as the Treasurer) to act as their agent. This agent, known as the 'signing agent', can then collect benefit payments on behalf of all claimants who use the alternative agency. Unlike a normal agent, the signing agent obtains payment by signing the order book as if he or she were the claimant. This means that the claimants no longer have control over their pension books, but the agent must give them the full amount of benefit due to them.

Who is responsible for abuse by an agent?

If you are acting as an agent and you lose or otherwise misappropriate the money, you are liable to make good the loss. There is no liability on the Benefits Agency or anyone else. If you do not refund the money, the claimant can take legal proceedings against you or you could face possible prosecution.

There is no provision to regulate or monitor the use of agency in the collection of benefits, so it is important that claimants understand what they are doing in using an agent and only nominate someone whom they know is trustworthy. If you suspect that someone who is acting as an agent is not acting properly, you should tell the claimant and complain to the Benefits Agency.

Powers of Attorney

The previous section described some of the informal arrangements that can be made by people who need help in dealing with financial matters. In addition, there are more formal measures that can be taken by people who wish to delegate responsibility for some, or even all, of their financial affairs to someone else. This is done by making a power of attorney.

What is a power of attorney?

A power of attorney is a particular sort of agency (see p 13). When people make a power of attorney, what they (the donors) are doing is completing a legal document appointing another person (an attorney) to act on their behalf in the management of property and financial affairs. A power of attorney can be general or can be limited to specific powers.

If you have been asked to act as an attorney, a power of attorney provides you with a legal document that you can show to other people (eg officials in banks, building societies and Benefits Agency offices) to prove that you have been authorised to act on behalf of the donor and to show the extent of your powers.

Who can make a power of attorney?

People who are both capable and entitled to do a particular transaction can hand the job over to someone else by making a power of attorney. Generally, we say that people are capable of doing something if they understand what the task involves and what consequences are possible. They are capable of making a power of attorney if they understand what the effects of delegating that task or tasks might be. They do not need to understand the technicalities of how to carry out the tasks.

The following are examples of individuals who might wish to make a power of attorney and are likely to be capable of doing so.

- People who go abroad for long periods and want someone to look after their affairs while they are away.
- People who are physically disabled and, as a result, find it difficult to handle their own affairs (eg because of limited mobility).
- People who are becoming forgetful and who decide that they need help in managing their affairs. So long as they are quite aware of what they are doing, they can still make a power of attorney.
- People who would like to make provision for a time when they may become incapable of managing their own affairs – they can make an enduring power of attorney (see p 25).

A **power of attorney** cannot be made by people who are not mentally capable of understanding what they are doing. Similarly, an ordinary power of attorney (see p 23) that was made when the donor was mentally capable will automatically become invalid if the donor later loses the mental capacity to manage his or her own affairs. People who wish to arrange for an attorney to take over even if they become mentally incapable must make an **enduring power of attorney** (see p 25), which is a special legal document with additional safeguards.

Who can be an attorney?

Donors can choose anyone they like to be their attorney, with the exception of someone who is a child under 18 years or a person who is mentally incapable of managing money. What is vital is that donors choose someone they can trust, usually a close relative or friend. Donors whose affairs are particularly complicated may wish to appoint a professional attorney such as a solicitor or accountant, although professional attorneys will charge for their services. In all cases, agreement should be sought from the proposed attorney before taking steps to make the appointment, because an unwilling attorney cannot be forced to act.

It is advisable for donors to tell close relatives or friends that they intend to make a power of attorney, especially an enduring power, and to explain their choice of attorney. This may reduce the risk of conflict at a later stage between other family members who might think that they should have been chosen as attorney instead. It will also help to confirm that donors are making the choice themselves, and are not being put under pressure by others.

Can there be more than one attorney?

Donors can appoint as many attorneys as they wish, but they must make clear whether they wish the attorneys to act 'jointly' or 'jointly and severally'.

If you have been appointed as one of two (or more) **joint attorneys,** you must always act together with the other attorney(s), and the agreement or signature of all attorneys must be obtained before any transaction can be carried out. This is often used as a safeguard against possible fraud or abuse by one attorney. However, if one of the joint attorneys dies or becomes mentally incapacitated, the power of attorney will no longer be valid; if one attorney is unavailable, it will be ineffective.

If you have been appointed as one of **joint and several attorneys,** this gives you and the other attorney(s) the power to act either independently or together. Your signature or any action you take alone would be as valid as if you were the sole attorney. In this case the death or mental incapacity of one of the attorneys would not make the power of attorney invalid, and the surviving attorney(s) may continue to act.

For example, within a family, if one elderly parent has died, the best arrangement may be for the surviving parent (the donor) to appoint two or more of their (now adult) children to be joint and several attorneys, and for those children to have an understanding that they will always act jointly, unless circumstances make this impracticable. Alternatively, the donor may choose to appoint a professional (such as a solicitor) to act jointly and severally with a family member, so that the relative can deal with day-to-day matters and the professional can deal with more complex issues.

Responsibilities of the attorney

If you are acting as an attorney, you must do only the things you have been authorised to do. If you have been asked to use a particular method to carry out a task, you should try to use that method. You cannot delegate any duties unless you are authorised to do so.

In particular, you must do the following:

- Use the same degree of care and skill as if you were conducting your own affairs.

- If you are a paid attorney, acting in the course of your profession, exercise proper professional competence.
- Act in good faith, if possible informing the donor of any conflict(s) of interest that may exist or may arise.
- Keep the donor's money in a separate bank or building society account and do not mix it with your own.
- Keep separate up-to-date accounts of the donor's financial affairs.

Can donors still act for themselves?

After making a power of attorney, donors can continue to act for themselves, either separately or together with the attorney(s), for as long as they are capable of doing so. The making of a power of attorney does not deprive donors of the right or power to act personally, and they may cancel it at any time (eg if unhappy with the attorney's behaviour) as long as they are still capable of doing so.

What types of power of attorney are there?

There are three main types of power of attorney:

- an ordinary power of attorney (see pp 23–24);
- a trustee power of attorney (see pp 24–25);
- an enduring power of attorney (see pp 25–32).

The most commonly used are ordinary and enduring powers of attorney, which either can be drawn up in general terms, giving the attorney 'blanket' authority to act on the donor's behalf in all financial matters, or they can be limited to specific powers, with or without restrictions or conditions.

If you have been given a **general** power, you have complete authority to act on the donor's behalf in relation to financial matters. You have the power to do anything that the donor could have done (with a few exceptions described below), and you can ask for any information you need about the donor's financial affairs such as how much money the donor has in the bank or the value of the donor's property. You can also sign most legal documents on behalf of the donor without having to get permission each time.

The few exceptions to what you are allowed to do under a general power are as follows:

- You cannot sign a Will or codicil (an addition to an existing Will) for the donor.
- If the donor is an agent or an attorney for someone else, you cannot take over this role.
- You cannot act in situations that require the donor's personal knowledge (eg acting as a witness in court).
- You cannot force someone else to deal with you rather than the donor or to enter into a contract with you when you are acting on behalf of the donor.

A general power of attorney is simple to draw up, which is why it is often used even where such blanket authority is not strictly required. It is important for donors to consider whether it is really necessary to give an attorney these unlimited powers or if a limited power might be more suitable in the circumstances.

If you are acting under a **limited** power, you do not have complete authority. Rather, the power defines precisely what you are allowed to do on the donor's behalf, either by specifying particular acts (eg buying or selling property, transferring investments or just paying certain bills or fees) or by giving you authority to do everything except particular acts (eg everything except the sale of the donor's house), or by setting out a combination of such instructions.

Drawing up a limited power of attorney is a much more complicated affair than a general power, because the document must be written in precise terms. Powers of attorney are designed to be 'restrictively construed'. This means that, in the event of a dispute about the extent of a limited power of attorney, a court would probably decide that any powers that are ambiguous have not been delegated to the attorney. Also, if there is any ambiguity about your powers as the attorney, another person may refuse to accept that you have the right to act on the donor's behalf. You would also have the right to refuse to act even though the donor may wish you to do so.

If donors decide to grant a limited power of attorney, it is important that they consider whether any other arrangements need to be made for the management of the part of their affairs not covered by the power of attorney.

Ordinary power of attorney

An ordinary power of attorney is a deed (a particular form of legal document) whereby donors can appoint attorney(s), either on a temporary or a longer term basis, to act on their behalf in financial matters, while they are still capable of acting for themselves.

How to make an ordinary power of attorney

An ordinary power of attorney that is intended to give the attorney general powers can be drawn up by using a standard form of wording (see Appendix 1, p 144) or by completing a pre-printed form available from law stationers.

If limitations or restrictions are to be imposed on the attorney's powers, the document becomes more complicated, and should be drawn up in consultation with a solicitor.

In either case, it must be clearly stated on the document that it is intended to be a deed.

Signing an ordinary power of attorney

To make a power of attorney valid, it must be signed by the donor, and the signature must be witnessed and attested. This means that the donor signs first, then the witness signs a clause, called the 'attestation clause', which confirms that the donor signed the document in his or her presence. The witness does not need to know what the power contains. The witness (who should be at least 18 years of age) must not be either the attorney or the donor's married partner, and preferably not the attorney's married partner.

If the donor is physically disabled and therefore unable to sign the document, someone else can sign for the donor in his or her presence, but the signature must be confirmed by two witnesses. This is called 'signing by direction'. Special wording is needed on the document, so it would be wise to get a solicitor to deal with this.

The document should be kept by the attorney, to be produced as proof of his or her authority to act on behalf of the donor, if and when requested. If copies are needed, these must carry a certificate verifying each page of the document, signed by the donor or by a solicitor or stockbroker.

Validity of an ordinary power of attorney

A power of attorney can be limited to a specific period of time or it can be drawn up to run out after certain tasks have been completed. If there is no time limit specified in the power, it will remain valid until one of the following occurs:

- it is revoked (cancelled) either by the donor or the attorney or by a court order;
- the death of either the donor or the attorney;
- the bankruptcy of either the donor or the attorney;
- it is 'revoked by implication', ie something happens to make the power invalid, such as the donor becoming mentally incapable.

Legally, anyone dealing with the attorney is entitled to assume that the power of attorney remains valid unless and until notified that the power has ended. This applies whether the power has been ended by the donor or the attorney or by the incapacity or death of one of them. In practice, this means that if you are acting as an attorney, anything that you do after the power has ended will still be valid if neither you nor the person you are dealing with knew the power had ended.

How to revoke an ordinary power of attorney

A power of attorney may be revoked at any time, either by the donor cancelling the power or by the attorney refusing to continue to act. Revoking the power of attorney may be done verbally, but should preferably be done in writing and should be noted on the document itself. The person revoking the power should also notify anyone else concerned with the donor's affairs, such as banks and savings institutions, that the power has ended.

Trustee power of attorney

A trust is a legal 'instrument' by which someone can arrange for other people (trustees) to hold money or property, and use it on behalf of or for the benefit of others, according to the terms set out in the trust document, which may be a deed or a Will. For example, a Will or a deed may be drawn up in such a way as to give trustees discretionary powers, which means they can decide how best to use the income or capital for the benefit of a particular person (or persons). It is also possible for people to arrange for their own money or property to be held by trustees, who would then use it on their behalf according to the conditions set out in the trust.

Property that is owned by two or more people is held on trust. The joint owners are the trustees and are said to hold the 'legal estate in land' (ie the property) 'on trust'. Trustees cannot delegate their power to someone else by using an ordinary power of attorney.

An ordinary power of attorney is therefore not suitable for managing a donor's share of a property that is jointly owned with another person, as it would not give the attorney any right to deal with the donor's share and interest in such a property. A trustee power of attorney must be granted instead, under which the donor, as trustee, can authorise an attorney to carry out the trustee's functions for a short period, not exceeding twelve months. However, the trustee power ceases to be valid if the donor loses capacity (ie the donor becomes mentally incapable).

Alternatively, donors who are also trustees can make an enduring power of attorney (see below), which empowers an attorney to take over the trustee functions of any trust of which the donor is a trustee, both before and after the onset of incapacity.

How to make a trustee power of attorney

The law of trusts is extremely complicated. A trust and any related power of attorney should always be drawn up by a solicitor. It is not possible to give any further details here, and you are recommended to seek legal advice if you are a trustee or own property jointly with someone else.

Enduring power of attorney

An enduring power of attorney is a form of deed that enables donors, while still mentally capable, to appoint an attorney:

- *either* to take over their affairs at once and to continue to act as attorney when they become mentally incapable;
- *or* to act as attorney only when they are no longer mentally capable to act for themselves.

In either case, once the donor starts to become mentally incapacitated, the enduring power must be registered with the Public Trust Office under powers delegated by the Court of Protection. For more information about the Court of Protection and the Public Trust Office, see pages 41–56.

How to make an enduring power of attorney

An enduring power of attorney must be drawn up using a prescribed form, which has three parts (see Appendix 2, pp 145–148). The form is available from solicitors or from law stationers.

The form includes explanations of the consequences of making or accepting an enduring power of attorney, and these must always be present on the document. These explanatory notes must be read by, or to, donors – who must then agree to a statement printed on the form, that they intend the power to continue even after they become mentally incapacitated. Similarly, you, the attorney, must agree to a statement that you understand what actions you will need to take in these circumstances.

When completing the form, donors must state whether they wish the attorney(s) to have general authority to act on their behalf, or if they wish to put limitations or restrictions on the power (see pp 21–22). Donors wishing to make a limited enduring power would be wise to seek legal advice before completing the form.

Signing an enduring power of attorney

An enduring power of attorney must be signed and dated by both the donor (on Part B of the form) and the attorney(s) (on Part C), each in the presence of a witness, although not necessarily at the same time or with the same witness. The donor must sign first and must be mentally capable of understanding what the enduring power is and what it is intended to do. The attorney(s) can sign at any time later, as long as the donor is still mentally competent, otherwise the power will not be valid. Each attorney must complete a separate Part C, the additional sheets having been firmly attached to the document beforehand.

If the donor is physically unable to sign the enduring power, someone else can sign for the donor in his or her presence, but the signature must be confirmed by two witnesses, in the spaces provided on the form. This is called 'signing by direction', and a statement must be added to the form that it has been signed at the donor's direction. Alternatively, the donor can make a mark on the document in place of a signature – a thumbprint, a cross or some other form of personal mark is acceptable, so long as it is confirmed by the witness as being the donor's mark. A special clause must be added to the document, confirming the way in which the power was signed and stating that the power and explanatory information have been read over to the donor, who appeared to understand fully what was happening.

The choice of an independent witness is important, as this witness could be called upon later to give evidence of the donor's mental capacity to make an enduring power. The witness must not be the attorney or the donor's married partner, and preferably not the attorney's married partner.

Duties of the attorney(s) under an enduring power

If you are acting as attorney under an enduring power, you have the same responsibilities as any attorney (see p 20). But you also have additional duties to register the power with the Public Trust Office and to notify certain people once the donor begins to lose the mental capacity to manage property for himself or herself.

Registering an enduring power of attorney

If you have any reason to believe that the donor is or is becoming mentally incapable of managing his or her affairs, you must, as soon as practicable, apply to register the enduring power with the Public Trust Office. This is your decision, as no medical evidence is required by the Public Trust Office, but it is important that you do not take over the donor's affairs unnecessarily. If in doubt, the donor's family doctor may be able to advise you.

As soon as you have decided to make the application, your powers as the attorney are suspended until registration has taken place, although limited powers are available if you need to take emergency action. Consult a solicitor or ask for advice from the Public Trust Office, if you think urgent action is needed.

Notification

First of all, you must give notice to the donor and certain members of the donor's family of your intention to register the enduring power. This is so that they not only know what is happening but also have a chance to object if they feel that something is wrong – for example, if the donor is still capable of managing, or if the attorney is thought to be unsuitable.

You must give notice to the donor, to any co-attorney and to at least three of the donor's nearest relatives in the following order of priority:

- the donor's married partner (including separated but not divorced partners);
- the donor's children;
- the donor's parents;
- the donor's brothers and sisters (both full and half siblings);
- the widow or widower of a child of the donor;
- the donor's grandchildren;
- the children of the donor's full brothers and sisters;
- the children of the donor's half brothers and sisters;
- the donor's uncles and aunts;
- the children of the donor's uncles and aunts.

If there is more than one relative in a particular class of relatives who is entitled to be notified, you must give notice to all members of that class. For example, if the donor has four children, all four must be notified as well as the donor's married partner.

If the donor does not have three living relatives who fall within the above list, you should say so on the form when applying to register the enduring power. You do not need to give notice to:

- any relative whose name or address you do not know and have been unable to find out;
- any person you believe to be under 18 years or mentally incapable;

- yourself as the attorney (although you can count yourself towards those entitled to be notified).

If you believe the donor (or any relative) may be distressed by receiving the notice, or that giving notice is unlikely to serve any useful purpose, you can ask the Public Trustee (the Head of the Public Trust Office) to dispense with the requirement to give notice to that person. This dispensation is rarely granted, as it is the donor's right to be informed and to have other relatives notified, and to be given the chance to object. Dispensation will be given only when there is medical evidence that the donor would be harmed by the notice.

You must use Form EP1 (see Appendix 3, p 149) for all the notices. Copies of the form are available from the Public Trust Office or law stationers. You must hand the notice personally to the donor, offering any necessary explanation, but sending notices to relatives by first-class post is sufficient.

Registration

As soon as you have served all the required notices, you must send the application for registration to the Enduring Power of Attorney Team at the Public Trust Office (address on p 136). You must make the application on Form EP2 (see Appendix 4, p 151) and send it to the Public Trust Office with the original enduring power document and the registration fee (check with the Public Trust Office for the current amount). Cheques and postal orders should be made payable to the Public Trust Office. You will get this money back later from the donor's estate. In cases of hardship, the Public Trustee will consider requests to postpone or waive payment of the fee.

The completed application should be received by the Public Trust Office no later than ten days after the last notice has been given or permission has been given to dispense with notice, whichever is the later. It may be possible for you to get the time extended if necessary.

Once you have made the application for registration, you can use the donor's money to provide for his or her immediate needs and for anyone else who is dependent on the donor. If necessary, you can also take urgent action to prevent the donor losing money or property, but it is advisable to ask the Public Trust Office first.

On receiving the application, the Public Trust Office will check to ensure that everything is in order and will hold the papers for 35 days from the date you served the last notice. At the end of this time, if no objections have been received, and there are no other matters to be sorted out, the Public Trustee will register the enduring power.

If the Public Trust Office finds a defect in the power that cannot be rectified (eg the donor has failed to specify whether the attorneys should act jointly or jointly and severally), the power cannot be registered. If, by this time, the donor does not have capacity to make a new power, you may have to apply to the Court of Protection or the Public Trustee for some other authority to act on the donor's behalf (see pp 41–55).

What happens if someone objects to registration?

A member of the donor's family, or the donor him- or herself, may object to registration – for example, if they feel that the donor is still capable of handling his or her own affairs or that the attorney is unsuitable. The grounds for objection are set out in the notice Form EP1 (see Appendix 3, p 150).

If someone objects, a copy of the objection will be sent to you as the attorney or to your solicitor. If you and the objector cannot resolve the problem between yourselves, the Public Trust Office will refer the matter to the Court of Protection, which will probably set a date for a hearing to decide whether the objection is valid. The Court will direct who is to be given notice of the hearing and what further information or evidence the Court may require. At the hearing, the Court can decide any of the following:

- whether to register the power of attorney;
- if so, whether you should be given instructions on how to manage the donor's affairs in the way set out in the enduring power;
- whether you need to be supervised by the Court while you are acting as attorney.

Neither the Court nor the Public Trust Office has the power to appoint alternative or additional attorneys. If the Court decides not to register the power, either the donor will continue to manage his or her own affairs or, if the donor lacks capacity, an application must be made to the Court of Protection or to the Public Trustee for some other authority to act on the donor's behalf (see pp 41–55).

After registration

After the registration procedure has been completed, the enduring power document will be returned to you, stamped as registered and carrying the seal of the Public Trustee or the Court. You then have full authority to act as attorney, as set out in the document.

Under normal circumstances neither the Public Trust Office nor the Court will supervise your actions, but the Court does have the power to do so if necessary; for example, if there are allegations of abuse against you. You will also have to apply to the Court for authority if you need to take certain actions that were not specified in the enduring power.

Can registration be cancelled?

An application to cancel registration can be made to the Court of Protection by anyone who considers that it is no longer appropriate. The Court must cancel the registration if it is satisfied that any of the following applies:

- the donor is and is likely to remain mentally capable;
- the donor is bankrupt or has died;
- a sole or joint attorney is bankrupt, has lost mental capacity or has died;
- there was no valid enduring power of attorney;
- there was fraud or duress involved in making the power of attorney;
- the attorney is unsuitable.

Can an enduring power of attorney be revoked?

Before registration, an enduring power can be revoked by the donor at any time while still mentally capable. The attorney can also refuse to continue to act, and must so inform the donor.

Once registered, the power cannot be revoked by the donor. If you do not wish to continue to act as the attorney after the power has been registered, you must first notify the Public Trust Office and also inform the donor.

How long does an enduring power last?

Once registered, the enduring power of attorney will remain valid until one of the following occurs:

- the death or bankruptcy of the donor;
- the death, bankruptcy or mental incapacity of a sole or joint attorney;
- revocation by order of the Court of Protection.

Help and advice

If the donor has substantial money or property, or where there may be a conflict of interest (eg you are likely to be the main beneficiary when the donor dies), it is important that the donor seeks separate and independent legal advice before making a power of attorney.

The instructions to the solicitor to prepare a power of attorney, particularly an enduring power, must always be given by the donor, not the attorney, and the solicitor's duty remains to the donor, even after the donor loses capacity. Where there is no conflict of interest, you can continue to obtain advice from that solicitor, but if a conflict emerges, you should get independent advice from another solicitor.

Further information and advice about enduring powers of attorney can be obtained from the Customer Services Unit of the Public Trust Office (address on p 136). The Public Trust Office also produces a free explanatory booklet on enduring powers of attorney, details of which are given on page 138.

Formal Arrangements for Limited Income and Savings

The previous two sections described the arrangements people can make for themselves if they are having problems managing their own financial affairs. However, if they later become confused and mentally incapable of understanding what is going on, these arrangements will cease to be valid unless an enduring power of attorney (see p 25) has been made and can be registered.

We now look at what can be done to take over other people's financial affairs when they are no longer capable of making their own arrangements. They may not have asked for your help and you may find that you have to act without their consent or even against their wishes. This section describes the various formal arrangements that can be made for people who have a limited income and/or a small amount of savings. These include:

- managing Social Security benefits as appointee;
- collecting pensions and salaries as appointee;
- claiming tax refunds;
- dealing with small amounts of savings;
- dealing with life assurance.

In most other cases, particularly if the person you want to act for has a large income and considerable savings, it will be necessary for you to make an application to the Court of Protection to take over the management of his or her financial affairs (see pp 41–55).

Claiming Social Security benefits as appointee

For people who are entitled to a Social Security benefit or pension, but who are mentally incapable of managing their own affairs, the Secretary of State for Social Security (in practice the benefit supervisor in the local Benefits Agency office) can appoint someone else, called an 'appointee', to act on their behalf. The appointee can make claims, receive payments and spend the money on the claimant's needs.

How to apply for an appointment to be made

Anyone who thinks that someone who is receiving a benefit or pension is no longer capable of managing his or her own affairs can write to the local Benefits Agency office asking for an appointment to be made. The person applying does not have to be the proposed appointee. The person wishing to be appointed will usually be asked to complete Form BF 56.

How is the appointment made?

The Benefits Agency staff should first make enquiries, to satisfy themselves on the following:

- That the claimant is mentally incapable of handling his or her own affairs – the claimant should be visited, or, if a visit is not possible or is inconclusive, appropriate medical evidence should be obtained.
- Whether a receiver has been appointed by the Court of Protection with power to claim or receive payments on the claimant's behalf (see p 43).
- Whether there is a valid enduring power of attorney, authorising the attorney to claim or receive benefits for the claimant (p 25).
- That the proposed appointee takes an active interest in the claimant's welfare and is suitable and willing to act – the person should be visited and, if necessary, references taken up.

In the past, these enquiries have not always been carried out and sometimes only cursory investigations were made. However, steps are now being taken by the Benefits Agency to ensure that procedures are followed and that the claimant and prospective appointee are visited.

Who can be appointed?

The appointee can be an individual over the age of 18 (eg a friend or relative) or a professional person (eg a solicitor or local authority officer). However, people who cannot read or write, who are frail or confused, or who are known to be dishonest or unable to manage money are unlikely to be appointed.

The benefit supervisor of the Benefits Agency will decide who should be appointed and will usually take into account the following:

- Priority will normally be given to a close relative who lives with or frequently visits the claimant.
- If able to express a view, the claimant should be given the opportunity to choose or object to the appointee.
- If the claimant has previously made a power of attorney, the attorney should be appointed.
- If considered suitable, the person giving information to the Benefits Agency about the claimant's mental incapacity may be asked to act.
- If none of the above is possible, the claimant's next of kin and the person who gave the information will be asked to suggest who might be willing and suitable to act as appointee.
- If the claimant is in hospital and there is no relative or friend who can act as appointee, a hospital manager or administrative officer may be appointed.
- If the claimant lives in a residential or nursing home and there is no one else who can act as appointee, the manager or proprietor of the home may be appointed as a last resort, but this is to be avoided when at all possible, to prevent the risk of abuse (eg using the money for the benefit of other residents rather than just the claimant).

Responsibilities of the appointee

If you have been made an appointee, you have the right to act as if you were the claimant. You can make a claim for any benefit the claimant is entitled to, make statements to the Benefits Agency about the claimant's circumstances, and receive and deal with any payments. You have a duty to report any changes that would affect the claimant's benefit, and you have the same rights of appeal as though you were yourself the claimant.

The benefit remains in the claimant's name, and any money you receive on behalf of the claimant must be used solely for the claimant's needs, comfort and well-being.

You have no right to use or spend the claimant's capital, unless the capital is made up of a limited amount of accumulated Social Security benefits. If you need to deal with other capital or large amounts of savings, you should ask the Public Trust Office (address on p 136) if an application should be made to the Court of Protection (see pp 41–55). The Public Trust Office has suggested that further authority is unlikely to be needed where the accrued savings amount to no more than one month's accommodation costs, plus (say) a £500 cash float to meet unforeseen circumstances.

Where an appointee is acting for several claimants (eg for claimants in residential or nursing home care or hospital), the Benefits Agency should make clear to the appointee that money intended to cover claimants' individual needs must not be used for other purposes. There have been instances where the proprietor of a residential or nursing home has acted as appointee for all the residents and pooled the claimants' personal money into a common fund to be used for the needs of all of them (eg to buy equipment for the residential home), even though the claimants were not able to agree to this. If you suspect this is happening, you should report it to the Benefits Agency.

Can the appointment be cancelled?

Your appointment can be revoked (cancelled) at any time if the Benefits Agency believe that you have not been using the claimant's money solely in his or her interests.

The benefit supervisor will normally interview you first to find out what has been going on and to point out your duties as an appointee. If you are a close relative and you agree to use the claimant's money appropriately in future, it is likely that your appointment will be continued for a trial period.

How long does the appointment last?

Your appointment will last until one of the following occurs:

- the claimant recovers and is able to act for him- or herself;
- you resign from your appointment;
- a receiver is appointed by the Court of Protection;
- you or the claimant dies.

Collecting pensions and salaries as appointee

Similar arrangements for appointeeship can be made for people who are mentally incapable of managing their own money, who receive a pension, salary, superannuation allowance or other work-related payment from any of the following:

- a government department;
- the armed forces;
- Members of Parliament pension fund;
- Church of England clergymen's pension fund;
- some local authority pension funds (but the maximum payable in any one year is limited).

The relevant department or pension fund will need to see medical evidence that the person entitled to the payment is mentally incapacitated. An arrangement can then be made for them to pay all or part of the money to an appointee, usually a carer or close relative, to be used solely for the person's benefit. Any funds remaining may be used for the benefit of family or other people for whom the person may be expected to provide, or to reimburse people who have helped to pay any debts.

If the person entitled to the pension is in a residential care home or other institution, payment can be made to that institution, but the same conditions for the use of the money will apply.

In the case of pensions for Church of England clergy and for local authority employees, the Court of Protection must be informed if arrangements are made for payment to an appointee.

Problems with appointeeship

In paying money to an appointee, there is always some risk of people being deprived of the right to control what little money they have because of the lack of any effective safeguard. Neither the Benefits Agency nor the departments and organisations referred to above have the resources to be able to monitor or check that appointees are acting properly.

If you are acting as an appointee, you should take your responsibilities seriously and keep careful records of what you spend the money on.

Not only will this protect you against wrongful allegations of misman-agement or abuse, but it will also help to reassure the person you are acting for.

Complaints against an appointee

The Benefits Agency and other organisations depend on reports from relatives or friends of claimants and from caring agencies, health care workers or solicitors to inform them if appointees are failing in their obligations to the claimant. That being the case, they can then take action to cancel the appointment and set about finding someone more suitable and trustworthy.

If you are worried about an appointee who is acting for someone else, you should report your concerns to the relevant department and ask them to investigate. Remember that claimants are rarely in a position to be able to complain for themselves.

Claiming tax refunds

It is possible for tax refunds below a certain amount to be paid to the next of kin of people who are mentally incapable of managing their own affairs. Applications for repayment should be made to the relevant tax office, setting out the reasons for payment to be made to the next of kin, if possible enclosing medical evidence.

The limits are reviewed from time to time, and details of the current limits can be obtained from the Inland Revenue. If the refund is over the set limits, repayment will only be made to a receiver appointed by the Court of Protection (see p 43) or to the holder of a registered enduring power of attorney (see p 27).

Dealing with small amounts of savings

In general, it is not possible to use the savings of people who are not capable of giving their consent, unless you have been authorised to do so either under an enduring power of attorney or by authorisation of the Court of Protection or the Public Trustee.

For account holders who have only a small amount of savings that they cannot manage for themselves, some banks and building societies may allow withdrawals in certain circumstances, and may arrange limited facilities for you to use the account to provide for the immediate needs of the account holder.

However, if the savings are safely invested (eg in Savings Certificates or cash on deposit at the National Savings Bank) and the person you are acting for does not at present need to use them, all that you have to do is to ensure that bank books and other documents are kept in a safe place.

It is difficult to specify the circumstances in which you would be allowed to use someone else's account, as different banks and building societies have different policies. You should write to the relevant branch where the person you are acting for has an account, setting out the circumstances and what facilities you require. If there is any problem, you should contact the head office of the particular bank or building society.

The bank or building society is entitled to refuse your request to use another person's account. However, if they refuse, you can make an application to the Public Trust Office for permission to use the account, either by means of a Direction or Short Order or by being appointed receiver by the Court of Protection, as described in the next section (see pp 41–55).

Dealing with life assurance

If the person whose affairs you are handling has a life assurance policy and has previously made arrangements to surrender or renegotiate the policy (see p 80), the insurance company may agree to pay some of the policy money to you. The insurance company has discretion to deal with policy money up to a certain limit; check with the company for details of the current limit.

However, the company cannot be forced to deal with you unless you have been authorised by the Court of Protection or Public Trustee (see p 41) or are acting under a registered enduring power of attorney (see p 27). You will certainly need this authority if you wish to surrender the policy on behalf of the person you are acting for, but you should first seek independent financial advice.

Other arrangements

There may be other instances in which proceedings in the Court of Protection are not essential for you to take control over an aspect of the financial affairs of someone who is mentally incapable. It is best to seek advice from the Customer Services Unit of the Public Trust Office, which will tell you whether it is necessary to apply to the Court. If an application is not required, they may be able to suggest other arrangements you can make.

The Court of Protection

The Court of Protection and the Public Trust Office

The Court of Protection looks after and manages the financial affairs of people who, because of mental disorder, are unable to manage for themselves. The Court of Protection is an office of the Supreme Court and also a court of law, which decides disputes and makes decisions about financial matters affecting people who lack capacity to make their own decisions.

The people who come within the Court's jurisdiction are referred to in the law as 'patients'. This is the term used here for the sake of clarity, even though it is somewhat outdated. Patients may also be referred to as 'people who lack capacity' or 'incapacitated'.

The Public Trust Office is an Executive Agency within the Lord Chancellor's Department. The Chief Executive of the Agency is also the Public Trustee and Accountant General of the Supreme Court. The services provided by the Public Trust Office are governed by Citizen's Charter standards.

Some of the Court's functions have been formally delegated to the Public Trustee, although the Court retains the power to carry out any of those delegated functions itself. The administration of the Court's decisions is carried out by various divisions of the Public Trust Office, mainly the Protection Division and the Receivership Division. Any enquiries, whether from the public or from legal advisers, should initially be addressed to the Customer Services Unit of the Public Trust Office (address on p 136), who will direct the enquirer to the relevant division.

What is mental disorder?

Mental disorder is defined in the law as including 'mental illness, arrested or incomplete development of mind, psychopathic disorder and any other disorder or disability of mind'.

Most of the Court's work is concerned with older people who have become progressively more confused and can no longer deal with their own affairs. However, the Court also acts for people with other types of mental disorder, including children and adults with learning disabilities, people who have suffered brain damage and those suffering from acute mental illness.

When is it necessary to involve the Court?

The Court of Protection need only be involved if none of the powers described in the preceding sections (pp 18–40) can be used. However, when action has to be taken to protect an incapacitated person's money or property or to use these for his or her benefit, it will usually be necessary to involve the Court.

The Court will need to be satisfied, after considering medical evidence, that the person is incapable of managing and administering his or her property and affairs by reason of mental disorder. Many people find they cannot manage money, though not because of mental disorder, while there are other people who do suffer from mental disorder but are quite capable of managing. In order for the Court to intervene, there must be medical evidence of mental disorder that causes an inability to manage property and financial affairs.

What are the main powers of the Court?

The Court can do, or can authorise someone else to do, anything that is 'necessary or expedient' in the management of a patient's property and financial affairs. This includes:

- Looking after the day-to-day needs of patients and members of their families, and any other people for whom patients might be expected to provide.
- Ensuring that patients are comfortably provided for and that their money is spent for their own benefit.
- Looking after the patients' affairs as they themselves would, if they were well enough.

How does the Court perform its duties?

There are four ways in which the Court can authorise the management of a patient's affairs.

- By the registration with the Public Trust Office of an enduring power of attorney made by the patient while still mentally competent (see pp 25–32).
- By granting a Receivership Order, which appoints a receiver to deal with the patient's affairs (see below).
- By making a Short Order, authorising someone to deal with the patient's affairs in a particular way (see p 52).
- When the patient does not have much money (less than £5,000) or property, by delegating to the Public Trustee the power to make a Direction authorising someone to use the patient's means appropriately (see p 53).

Applying to the Court

The procedures for applying to the Court are similar, whether a Receivership Order, a Short Order or a Direction of the Public Trustee is required. All initial inquiries should be made to the Customer Services Unit of the Public Trust Office (address on p 136), who will advise on the procedures to be followed and send the appropriate application forms. The Public Trust Office also publishes a free booklet called *Making an Application* which sets out the application procedures. These are described below.

Appointing a receiver

A receiver is a person appointed by the Court to deal with the day-to-day management of the patient's financial affairs. This includes claiming and collecting income, paying bills, looking after property and generally acting in the patient's interests in financial matters.

Anyone who considers that someone they know needs help in dealing with their financial affairs can apply to the Court of Protection. The person making the application does not have to be the proposed receiver.

Who can be appointed as receiver?

The Court has wide discretion as to whom it can appoint as receiver, but it must take into account the wishes of the patient, so far as possible. It is important that the person appointed as receiver has the confidence of the patient.

The receiver will usually be a close relative or friend of the patient. If that is not possible or if the patient's affairs are particularly complicated, a professional adviser such as a solicitor or accountant can be appointed, but they will usually charge fees for acting as receiver. Sometimes an officer of the local authority will agree to act as receiver. The Court must take account of the factors involved in each individual case (eg the cost to the patient, any potential conflicts of interest) and decide whom to appoint as receiver, based on what the Court considers to be in the patient's best interests.

In exceptional cases, if there is no one suitable or willing to be appointed as receiver or if there is family friction, the Court can appoint the Public Trustee. The disadvantage of using the Public Trustee, however, is that the fees are higher than when using a private receiver.

In cases of doubt as to who should be receiver, it is best to discuss it with members of the patient's family or with a solicitor, or to seek advice from the Public Trust Office.

Can there be more than one receiver?

Although this is possible, the Court is unlikely to approve the appointment of more than one receiver, as this tends to cause delay and inconvenience. If an application is made for joint receivers, it should be made clear which one is preferred if the Court refuses to appoint joint receivers.

How to apply for a receivership order

The following sections are written for people applying to be appointed as receivers.

Your first step is to write to the Customer Services Unit of the Public Trust Office (address on p 136), explaining the situation and asking for application forms. Alternatively, you can ask a solicitor to prepare the necessary forms and make the application. Either way, the following forms must be completed.

Two copies of the application form (Form CP 1)   This asks for your details and those of the patient and a description of your relationship (if any) with the patient.

The medical certificate (Form CP 3)   This form, together with the accompanying explanatory notes and return envelope must be sent for completion by the patient's doctor, or by a geriatrician or psychiatrist who has seen the patient recently. The doctor giving the certificate will return it direct to the Public Trust Office. If you cannot get a doctor to complete the form, the Court can ask one of the Lord Chancellor's Medical Visitors (see p 50) to interview the patient and report to the Court, but such visits are usually made only as a last resort or if there is a dispute between doctors about the patient's mental capacity.

The certificate of family and property (Form CP 5)   This asks questions about the patient's financial resources, property, debts and liabilities, and for details of the patient's family and dependants. All of the patient's financial affairs should be included, but if all the details are not available, these can be sent in later.

You should also give the name, address and occupation of someone to whom the Court can write for a reference as to your fitness and suitability to act as receiver. You cannot use as a referee relatives, your bank manager or a solicitor who is acting for you or the patient.

All of the above documents should be returned to the Public Trust Office, together with a copy of the patient's Will (if available), any original power of attorney made by the patient, and the 'commencement fee' – the Public Trust Office will tell you the current amount. The fee can eventually be repaid to you out of the patient's funds. If you cannot afford to pay the fee, you can ask for payment of the commencement fee to be postponed until money becomes available. If the patient has a low income, no fee is payable.

If any of the patient's affairs has to be dealt with urgently, a covering letter should be sent with the application forms, explaining what needs to be done (see also 'Emergency applications', p 47).

Is Legal Aid available?

Note that Legal Aid is *not* available for any proceedings in the Court of Protection. If you have asked a solicitor to make the application, the solicitor's costs will usually be paid from the patient's funds later on.

Notifying the patient

On receipt of the forms, the Court or your solicitor will arrange for a letter of notification to be given to the patient, usually in person by you, or by a doctor, nurse or solicitor known to the patient. The patient must be notified at least ten days before a decision is made by the Court, unless the Court has dispensed with (set aside) the requirement to notify the patient. However, it is rare for the Court to decide that the patient should not be notified and will do so only if there is medical evidence that it would cause harm or distress to the patient. If this is the case, you should ask the doctor to comment on it when completing Form CP 3 (see p 45).

The letter of notification explains why the application has been made, by whom, when the application will be considered by the Court and what steps are proposed. It encourages patients to write to the Court or telephone if they have any objections to the proposals. If necessary, someone else may contact the Court at the request of the patient.

Notifying others

If you are related to the patient and have made the application, you must inform all other relatives who are either equally or more closely related to the patient than you are.

If the application has been made by someone who is not a member of the family, the following relatives must be notified by the applicant:

- the patient's husband or wife;
- the patient's parents;
- the patient's brothers and sisters;
- the patient's children.

If no such relatives exist, any other known relatives should be notified.

If it is not practicable for all the above relatives to be notified, the Court will advise you on who should be notified.

When you fill in the certificate of family and property (Form CP 5), you must complete the section asking for details of who has been notified.

Emergency applications

In cases of extreme urgency, the Court can use any of its powers – including the appointment of an interim receiver – before the necessary medical evidence is available and without having to notify the patient or others. The Court must have reason to believe that the patient may be incapable of managing his or her affairs and that it is necessary to take urgent action to safeguard the person's money or property. You should send in the application forms and the certificate of family and property, and explain the need for urgency in a covering letter.

It is a good idea to telephone the Public Trust Office first, to check whether an emergency application is appropriate.

Arrangements for the hearing

After receiving the completed application the Court will normally set a hearing date within the next few weeks, when it will decide whether a receiver should be appointed. It is not usual for anyone to attend the hearing, but the Court can ask for anyone who is involved to attend. If someone wishes to challenge the appointment of a particular person as receiver, he or she can write to the Court and/or attend the hearing to make representations to the Court, but should let the Court know in advance of the intention to attend.

At the hearing the Court has four options:

- To make a First General Order, appointing a receiver (see below).
- To make a Short Order (see p 52).
- To adjourn the hearing until all the information required by the Court is to hand. (This may involve making further inquiries if objections have been raised by the patient or relatives.)
- To dismiss the application.

First General Order

If the Court is satisfied with all the information presented and considers that it is necessary to appoint a receiver, it will make a First General Order, appointing you as receiver.

The First General Order sets out your specific powers as receiver, which will depend on the patient's circumstances and how much money and property he or she has. The Court will prepare a draft of the order, and send it to you or your solicitor for approval. Sometimes the Court may request further information before the order can be finalised.

Once the First General Order has been settled, you can ask to be sent a number of sealed (stamped with the official seal) office copies of the order, which you can then register with institutions such as banks, building societies etc, to prove that you have been appointed receiver.

Is there a right of appeal?

Any person who is dissatisfied with a decision of the Court of Protection has the right to appeal within eight days of the decision being made. It is best to seek advice either from the Public Trust Office or from a solicitor for help with an appeal.

Will the receiver get paid?

If you have been appointed as a receiver, you will not be paid for your services, but you can charge for reasonable expenses (eg postage and travel), and these can be taken from the patient's money. If professional help or advice is required, you must get approval from the Court before incurring additional fees.

Is any form of security required?

Both as a business precaution and to make sure you do not mishandle the patient's affairs, the Court will normally require you to take out a security bond with an insurance company. The Court will prepare the security bond, and will provide a list of companies approved by the Court. The bond is like an insurance policy, with the annual premium payable out of the patient's funds. The sum insured is fixed by the

Court in proportion to the patient's annual income and is reviewed from time to time.

Powers of a receiver

As a receiver you can do all the things in relation to the property and financial affairs of the patient that the Court orders or authorises. The Public Trust Office issues free of charge a booklet on the *Duties of a Receiver* and a *Handbook for Receivers* with an alphabetical reference guide. These will be sent to you automatically when you are appointed receiver.

Generally speaking, you are responsible for the patient's income and must collect it from all sources and pay it into a special bank or building society account, which you must open in your name 'as receiver for [*patient's name*]'. You must then use it to pay the patient's maintenance costs and settle the patient's debts. Any surplus must be used for the patient's benefit.

Your specific powers are set out in the First General Order by which you were appointed. You may also be given additional powers by further orders, directions or authorisations given by the Court or the Public Trustee.

However, you do not have power over the 'person' of the patient, which means that you cannot decide such things as where the patient should live, give consent to medical treatment or stop the patient from socialising or getting married.

When must authority to act be obtained from the Court?

In the majority of cases, the Court is involved only in the appointment of a receiver and most subsequent directions are given by the Public Trustee, as an administrative rather than a judicial decision. The caseworker assigned to the patient's case at the Public Trust Office will advise you on the necessary procedures and will refer any matters requiring the Court's attention.

You must obtain specific authority from the Public Trustee before you can carry out any of the following on the patient's behalf:

- using the patient's savings or capital;
- making loans or gifts;
- buying or selling property;
- granting or giving up leases or tenancies;
- varying any authorised allowances (eg maintenance payments);
- varying the patient's investments;
- incurring an overdraft;
- taking or defending legal proceedings;
- entering into a deed of covenant.

You should write to the Public Trust Office explaining what is needed and why you think it is in the patient's best interests. The Public Trust Office will decide whether the matter should be referred to the Court or will make a decision, if necessary after further investigations, and issue you with any order or authority that it considers to be appropriate or necessary in the circumstances.

The Lord Chancellor's Visitors

There are three types of Visitors, all appointed by the Lord Chancellor, to assist the Court and the Public Trust Office in carrying out their duties.

Medical Visitors are senior consultant psychiatrists, who visit patients for specific purposes on the direction of the Court.

The **Legal Visitor** is a senior qualified legal adviser.

General Visitors visit certain groups of patients at regular intervals during the course of the receivership, to advise the Court on the patient's circumstances, and to see that all the reasonable needs of the patient are being met.

You can ask for a visit, especially if there is an urgent or special need, for example to discuss a particular major decision such as whether it is appropriate to ask the Public Trustee for authority to sell the patient's home. Also, the Court may request a visit to find out a particular fact or to carry out investigations. However, many patients will not receive a visit at all, unless the Court wants a particular investigation to be made. Neither you nor the patient should do anything to stop or obstruct the Visitor.

The Visitor's report is strictly confidential to the Court unless there are exceptional circumstances.

Fees

Fees are payable in respect of all matters dealt with by the Court of Protection and all administration carried out by the Public Trust Office. The fees are set by Parliament on a fixed scale, which is unrelated to the complexity of the patient's affairs or the amount of work carried out by the Public Trust Office. A pamphlet called *Fees*, available from that office, lists the current rates.

In addition to the commencement fee (see p 45), an annual 'administration fee' is payable, on the anniversary of the order appointing a receiver; it is based on the patient's annual income.

A further fee, called a 'transaction fee', is payable for every transaction that has to be authorised by the Court or the Public Trustee (see p 49).

What happens if the patient cannot afford to pay?

If a patient's income is less than £1,000 a year, or if he or she is receiving Income Support (see p 62), generally no fees are payable.

In other cases, the Public Trustee can postpone or waive the collection of all or part of any fee if payment might cause hardship to the patient or to his or her dependants, or if there are other exceptional circumstances. However, because the Protection Division of the Public Trust Office is required to cover its operating costs from patients' fees, this does not often happen.

Receivership accounts and annual enquiries

You will have to submit accounts of all receipts and payments you have made as receiver when requested by the Public Trust Office, usually on an annual basis. The First General Order (see p 48) will specify the period to be covered by the first account. The account forms will be sent to you shortly before the account is due, specifying what supporting information you should send with the account.

In some cases, you may be asked to respond to an annual enquiry, instead of being asked to provide a detailed receivership account. You will still have to be able to give accurate information about the patient's affairs. The Public Trust Office issues factsheets (No 1: *Accounts* and No 2: *Annual Enquiry*) that explain the procedures involved.

If you fail to submit accounts or respond to an annual enquiry, you run the risk of being discharged and replaced. If this happens, the security bond you took out may be enforced to cover any loss to the patient, and the insurance company will look to you for the recovery of any funds.

Can a receiver be challenged?

If someone wishes to challenge your appointment as receiver or to complain about a particular action you have taken as the receiver, he or she should write to the Public Trust Office setting out the complaint and providing any available evidence. That office can investigate the complaint and, if necessary, can refer the matter to the Court, which can decide any of the following:

- To confirm or revoke your appointment as receiver.
- To approve the decision you made that is being challenged.
- To overrule your decision and order you to take specific action.

If the person who made the complaint is still dissatisfied, he or she has a right of appeal, first to ask the Court to review the decision and subsequently to appeal to a nominated judge in the High Court.

How long will receivership last?

The receivership will come to an end for one of the following reasons:

- The Court is satisfied, on the basis of medical evidence, that the patient has recovered and is once again able to manage his or her own affairs.
- You wish to retire from your appointment as receiver, or for some other reason it becomes necessary to appoint a new receiver.
- The patient dies.

A Short Order

If the patient's affairs are relatively simple and straightforward (eg there are limited assets), it is possible for the Court to decide that it is not necessary to appoint a receiver. Instead, the Court may decide to make a Short Order, containing a few directions authorising the patient's money or property to be used in a certain way for his or her benefit.

The person given such authority is normally the person making the application, and usually a close relative. For example, the Short Order may authorise that person to:

- use the patient's money held in bank or building society accounts;
- sign a tenancy agreement or nursing/residential home contract on behalf of the patient;
- pay any fees, nursing/residential home charges, debts or solicitor's costs;
- make arrangements for the safekeeping of documents and valuables;
- provide an account of how the patient's affairs are being dealt with.

The Court may make an annual enquiry to ensure that the order is being complied with, and may charge a fee.

A Direction of the Public Trustee

If an application for receivership has not already been made, it is possible to ask for a Direction to be made by the Public Trustee. This is usually done in cases where the total value of the patient's assets is less than £5,000 and the affairs to be managed are relatively straightforward and so the appointment of a receiver is not necessary.

A Direction of the Public Trustee can authorise the patient's money or property to be used in a certain way, for his or her benefit. The person given such authorisation is normally the applicant.

When is a Direction appropriate?

A Direction of the Public Trustee may be suitable where the patient's capital is made up of any of the following:

- cash savings held in bank, building society or National Savings Bank accounts;
- Premium Bonds, National Savings Certificates or National Savings Income Bonds;
- cash held by someone else (eg a relative, friend or by a hospital).

However, the patient's income should not include any of the following, which would require the oversight of a receiver:

- dividends from stocks and shares;
- income or capital from a trust;
- an occupational or other private pension or annuity where the gross income exceeds £1,200 per annum.

How to apply for a Direction of the Public Trustee

The procedure is similar to applying for receivership (see p 44), except that the application forms are slightly different. First, contact the Customer Services Unit of the Public Trust Office (address on p 136) and ask for the relevant application forms. These are issued with Factsheet 5, *Applying for a Direction of the Public Trustee*, which explains the necessary procedures.

The following forms will need to be completed:

- the application form (Form CP1 (PT));
- the medical certificate (Form CP3 (PT)), which should be sent to the patient's doctor for completion;
- the certificate of family and property (Form CP5 (PT)).

Send the completed forms to the Public Trust Office together with a letter setting out your proposals as to what decisions need to be made and how the patient's affairs should be dealt with, to the best advantage of the patient.

Unlike an application for receivership, there is no formal obligation on you to inform the patient's relatives of your intention to apply, although it may be advisable to do so. If the Public Trustee decides to make a Direction, the Public Trust Office will first provide you with a letter of notification, which you must deliver personally to the patient. The Public Trustee can dispense with this requirement on the grounds that notice might harm the patient, but this is rare (see p 46).

When all the required information is to hand, and at least ten days after the patient has been notified, the Public Trustee will write to you, setting out the proposed Direction for your approval. Once you have confirmed that the proposals are satisfactory, the formal Direction will be drawn up, 'sealed' (stamped with the official seal) and issued to you. You can then use the document to prove your authority to deal with the patient's affairs.

The Public Trustee may make an annual enquiry or ask you to submit accounts to ensure that the Direction is being complied with.

Involving the patient

Whether you are acting as receiver or under the authority of a Short Order or Direction, you should always try to consult with the patient on any matter concerning his or her financial affairs. If the patient is able to express an opinion, you should always find it out and make it known to the Public Trust Office, even when it conflicts with your own views, and particularly when it concerns anything about which the Court or the Public Trustee has been asked to make a decision.

Patients should always be encouraged to continue to deal with their own affairs so far as they are able to. For example, some patients may be capable of handling small amounts of money through a bank account in their own name. Permission should be sought from the Public Trust Office, and, if agreed, the appropriate arrangements made with a bank or building society. In some cases, the Public Trust Office may require a limit to be placed on the account and arrange for you to top up the balance as necessary.

In any event, you should try to be aware of the needs and wishes of the patient and to use the available funds for the patient's benefit (in the widest sense) during the patient's lifetime. This includes providing not only basic necessities but also other comforts that the patient might like such as chocolates, fresh fruit, alcoholic beverages or new clothes, cards or presents for others or even larger and more unusual things such as a special chair or bed or the installation of a chair-lift if the patient can afford it.

Can the patient make a Will?

The patient may make a Will if the Court or the Public Trustee is satisfied that he or she has 'testamentary capacity' (see p 107). You should inform the Public Trust Office if the patient is considering making a Will. If it is considered that the patient does not have the capacity to make a Will, the Court has power to make a 'statutory Will' for the patient, making any provision that the Court considers the patient would have wanted (see p 108).

Help and advice

Help and advice can always be obtained from the Customer Services Unit of the Public Trust Office (address on p 136). Details of the free booklets and factsheets issued by this office are given on pages 138–139.

It is also possible to get legal advice from a solicitor or to instruct a solicitor to make all applications to the Court of Protection or act as receiver if appointed by the Court. It is advisable to find a solicitor who has experience of this type of work. However, remember that Legal Aid is not available in the Court of Protection and that a solicitor will make a charge for his or her services, normally payable from the patient's funds.

What Needs to be Done?

Managing other people's money is much the same as managing your own. You should try to put yourself in the position of the person whose affairs you have taken over and use the money in the way you believe he or she would have used it. You must always try to use it wisely.

Your first consideration will be to make sure that the person whose money it is is properly looked after and provided for, as well as any family or dependants that person may have. You should also try to think about any particular needs he or she may have – for some new clothes, a walking aid, a new radio or television – if the money available stretches to such things. You should also try to remember special occasions, such as birthdays and anniversaries, and buy presents on the person's behalf, including for yourself, if appropriate.

Part 3 looks at the various practical matters you may have to deal with, pointing out the things you should check and look out for, depending on the particular circumstances you are dealing with. Some of these you may be familiar with from dealing with your own financial affairs; others you may not have come across before, so you may need to seek independent financial advice.

Please remember that this book can give only *general* guidance and then suggest other sources where you can obtain more detailed information and help.

Money Matters

Claiming and collecting income

In taking over the management of other people's financial affairs, the first thing to check is whether they are receiving all the income they are entitled to. This will include checking entitlement to state benefits and pensions as well as occupational or personal pensions.

You should also consider whether it is necessary or desirable to try to increase income, for example by re-investing savings, by careful tax planning or by using the value of an owner-occupied house as a means of securing income.

This section briefly examines all of these options. References are made to publications from Age Concern and other bodies for further information. Addresses of advice agencies and organisations that may be able to offer practical help are given on pages 130–137.

Occupational and personal pensions

Many people who have worked regularly as employees will receive an occupational pension from their former employer(s). Occupational pension schemes vary tremendously, each providing different types of benefits.

It would be wise to check with previous employers of the person whose affairs you are looking after, as there may be small amounts of pension not being paid because the employer has not been given the person's up-to-date address. The Pension Schemes Registry (address on p 136) can help trace these pension schemes.

People who do not have an occupational (or company) pension may have paid into a personal pension, provided by banks, building societies, life assurance companies and unit trust companies.

If you have any problems claiming these pensions, the Pensions Advisory Service (OPAS – formerly the Occupational Pensions Advisory

Scheme) may be able to help (see address on p 136) or they can put you in touch with other organisations to help you.

All income from state, occupational or private pensions is taxable. People who have an occupational pension and/or who have income from employment will generally be taxed under the Pay As You Earn (PAYE) scheme (see p 69). People not covered by PAYE, or those who also have other forms of income, will be taxed under the self-assessment scheme (see p 70).

Social Security benefits and pensions

The following paragraphs summarise the various state benefits and pensions available for older people, and outline the circumstances in which they may be payable. Further information can be found in *Your Rights* published each year by Age Concern England, which also gives details of the relevant leaflets produced by the Benefits Agency.

Retirement Pension

Retirement Pension is a taxable benefit paid to people who have reached pension age (at present 60 for women and 65 for men) and have paid enough National Insurance contributions during their working lives. People who are or were married may be able to claim a pension based on their partner's or ex-partner's National Insurance contributions.

Retirement Pension consists of a *basic pension* (which could be the full amount or a reduced amount, depending on the National Insurance contributions paid), plus, in some cases:

- *additional pension* for those who worked after April 1978 (the rules for this scheme will change for those reaching pension age after April 1999);
- *graduated pension* for those who worked between April 1961 and April 1975;
- an amount equal to the *age-related addition* to long-term Incapacity Benefit for people already receiving this within eight weeks of reaching pension age (see p 60).

Some people may qualify for an additional pension or graduated pension even if they are not entitled to the basic pension. People who worked after reaching their pension age may receive extra pension.

Over-80s Pension

This is a retirement pension paid to people aged 80 and over who have either no state retirement pension or only a small amount. It is non-contributory, which means you do not have to have paid National Insurance contributions to qualify, but has residency conditions. It is also taxable.

Widow's Pension

This taxable pension is paid to widows who have not retired and were aged between 55 and 64 when their husband died, and whose husband had paid enough National Insurance contributions. This will usually change to Retirement Pension when she reaches pension age, if she is receiving Widow's Pension at that time.

Christmas Bonus

A bonus of £10 is paid in the first week of December each year to people over pension age receiving the above pensions or certain other disability benefits.

Incapacity Benefit

Incapacity Benefit is paid to people who have been unable to work because of sickness or disability, if they have paid enough National Insurance contributions. It is payable at three rates, depending on how long the claimant has been unable to work. Only the short-term lower rate, payable for the first 28 weeks is tax-free. An age-related addition is also payable to people who become incapable of work before the age of 45 years.

Payment of Incapacity Benefit will normally stop for people who reach pension age; they will then draw Retirement Pension. However, those who previously received Invalidity Benefit (which preceded Incapacity Benefit) and were over pension age on 13 April 1995 can choose whether to claim Retirement Pension or to continue drawing Incapacity Benefit until the age of 65 for women and 70 for men. The pros and cons require a fairly complicated calculation, depending on the individual's taxable income and other circumstances, so you should seek advice on this from one of the organisations listed on pages 130–137.

Severe Disablement Allowance

Severe Disablement Allowance is a non-taxable benefit for very disabled people who have been unable to work for at least 28 weeks but who do not have enough National Insurance contributions to qualify for Incapacity Benefit. The qualifying conditions are complex. It cannot usually be claimed for the first time by a person over 65 years of age.

Attendance Allowance

Attendance Allowance is a non-taxable benefit intended to help with the costs of illness or disability. It is payable in addition to other benefits, for people aged 65 or over who are ill or disabled, either physically or mentally, and who need a lot of looking after. There is no upper age limit for Attendance Allowance, but people who become disabled before the age of 65 should claim Disability Living Allowance instead (see below).

To qualify, most people will have needed attention or supervision for at least six months – unless they are found to be terminally ill, when they will qualify immediately. Attendance Allowance is non-contributory but there are stringent qualifying conditions. It is payable at two weekly rates according to the degree of help required, and is paid because of need, not because the claimant is being looked after. Someone who lives alone and is not being cared for may still qualify. Many initial claims are refused, but later granted on review or appeal, so seek advice from one of the advice agencies listed on pages 130–137.

Disability Living Allowance

Disability Living Allowance (DLA) is payable to people who become ill or disabled, and make a claim, before the age of 65. It is non-contributory and is not affected by other income or savings. Disability Living Allowance has two parts:

- *DLA care component* for people who need help with personal care or supervision because of physical or mental illness or disability. This is payable at three rates, according to the amount of help required.
- *DLA mobility component* for people who need help in getting around or require guidance or supervision because of their disability. This is paid at two different rates.

The qualifying conditions for both components are complex and the application forms are long and detailed. One of the advice agencies listed on pages 130–137 will be able to help with claims for Disability Living Allowance.

Invalid Care Allowance

Invalid Care Allowance is claimed by carers, who must be under 65 years of age and are caring for a severely disabled person (eg a person in receipt of Attendance Allowance) for at least 35 hours a week. The carer must not earn more than a small amount per week after deduction of certain work expenses. He or she does not have to be a relative and may live apart from the person being cared for. The allowance does not depend on having paid National Insurance contributions but is taxable, and other Social Security benefits will be taken into account.

Income Support

Income Support is paid to people who are not in full-time work or required to be available for work, and whose income falls below a certain amount, to help with weekly basic living expenses. It is designed to top up income to a level set by the Government. It is non-taxable and does not depend on National Insurance contributions.

People with savings of over £8,000 (£16,000 if living in a residential or nursing home) do not qualify, and there are detailed regulations setting out how the weekly amount of benefit is calculated. When someone's entitlement to Income Support is being assessed, most other forms of income and savings will be taken into account. However, some types of income, including Attendance Allowance and Disability Living Allowance, are ignored. Similarly, some types of capital, such as the home the person lives in, are not taken into account.

The level of Income Support is based on a personal allowance, which varies according to the age and size of family, if any. Additional premiums are awarded to disabled people and people over 60, there being different rates according to the individual's circumstances and age. Mortgage interest payments and service charges may also be paid by Income Support in some circumstances.

People in receipt of Income Support may also qualify for other benefits such as Housing Benefit, Council Tax Benefit, free dental treatment, help with spectacles, and lump sum payments from the Social Fund (see below).

The Social Fund

The Social Fund provides lump sum payments or loans to people with low incomes in order to meet exceptional expenses. Any savings over £500 (or £1,000 for people aged 60 and over) will be taken into account. Payments are made as of right towards funeral costs, maternity expenses and amounts for fuel during a period of extremely cold weather, so long as certain conditions are fulfilled.

The following grants or loans are also available, but are discretionary – that is, they are not paid as of right even if people fulfil certain conditions, but rather the officials concerned can decide whether or not to pay, taking account of Government guidance. Also, they are subject to regional cash limits.

Community Care Grants are sometimes available to people receiving Income Support in order to help them to move out of, or stay out of, institutional or residential care, and to continue to live in the community. Grants can also be paid to assist families who are under exceptional pressure or to enable someone on Income Support to visit a sick relative (in hospital or elsewhere) or attend a relative's funeral. The grants are directed at priority groups, which include people with mental or physical disability or illness or general frailty. They are given at the discretion of Social Fund Officers at the local Benefits Agency office and do not have to be repaid.

Budgeting Loans are discretionary and will only be given to people who have been receiving Income Support for more than 26 weeks, and only if they can be repaid later.

Crisis Loans are interest-free loans for emergency needs only, and will only be given if they can be repaid.

Housing Benefit

Housing Benefit gives help with paying rent for people with a low income and savings of not more than £16,000. It is paid by local authorities although the rules are set by the Government. Housing Benefit is non-taxable and does not depend on National Insurance contributions.

Council, housing association and private tenants can get help with rent and service charges, unless the landlord is a close relative and the household is shared or there is no commercial arrangement. Home owners cannot get help with mortgage payments or service charges, although these may be covered by Income Support.

Council Tax Benefit

Local authorities can provide financial assistance to help people to pay their Council Tax. There are two types of benefit:

- **Main Council Tax Benefit,** payable to the person responsible for paying Council Tax if they are on a low income and have savings of less than £16,000.
- **Second Adult Rebate,** available to some people who have one or more adults with low incomes living with them, regardless of their own income and savings.

The amount of Council Tax Benefit is worked out by the local authority according to rules set by the Government.

Some properties are exempt from Council Tax altogether – for example, if they are empty because the owner is living in residential care or with relatives. The amount of Council Tax due may also be reduced if discounts are given (eg for people who live alone or who are mentally impaired) or if alterations were made to the property or if it has certain features to meet the needs of a disabled person (eg extra space for a wheelchair). Further information is available in Age Concern Factsheet 21, *The Council Tax and older people.*

Independent Living Fund

The Independent Living Fund is a discretionary fund to help severely disabled people who need to pay for personal care or household services in order to remain living in the community. There are now two parts of the Fund:

- The **Independent Living (Extension) Fund,** which continues to make payments to people already receiving help from the Fund at the end of March 1993.
- The **Independent Living (1993) Fund,** which makes payments to new applicants who must be under 66 years of age.

Applicants to the 1993 Fund must be getting the highest care component of the Disability Living Allowance (see p 61), and must be on a low income with savings of less than £8,000. They must also be receiving a minimum level of services from the local authority but still need additional care (see p 87).

Direct payments

Since April 1996, local authorities have been able to give some disabled people money (called direct payments) instead of – or as well as – providing services. Individuals must use this money to organise and buy the personal care or services that the local authority has assessed them as needing (see p 88). Not all disabled people are entitled to direct payments, and local authorities also have discretion to refuse direct payments to anyone they judge would not be able to manage them. A person can have assistance in managing the direct payment but has the final responsibility of how the money is spent. At present, direct payments cannot be made to anyone over 65 unless they were receiving them before their 65th birthday. This age limit may be reviewed.

Re-investing for income

If the person you are acting for has investments but receives only a restricted income, it may be desirable, depending on the person's needs, to re-invest some of the money so as to produce more income. This is considered in more detail under 'Managing savings and investments' on page 72.

Raising income or capital from the home

If the person you are acting for owns his or her own home, it may be possible to use the value of the home to raise income or capital. In order to do this on behalf of another person, you will normally have to be acting under a power of attorney or by order of the Court of Protection or under a Direction of the Public Trustee (see Part 2 for details).

The schemes available for raising money from the value of the home are complicated and can be risky. You must get independent financial and legal advice before entering into a scheme, particularly on behalf of someone else. Age Concern England publishes a factsheet on the main schemes available (38, *Treatment of the former home as capital for people in residential and nursing homes*), as well as a book, *Using Your Home as Capital*, which is updated annually (see p 140). The main schemes are:

- **Home Income Plans,** sometimes called mortgage annuity or equity-release schemes, whereby an interest-only loan is raised on a proportion of the value of the property, which is used to buy an annuity to provide a monthly income for life. The home owner pays interest on the loan, but the amount of the loan itself is repaid only on the death of the home owner or when the house is sold.
- **Home Reversion Schemes,** whereby the home, or part of the home, is sold to a private company, called the reversion company, for a lump sum or an annuity income. The occupant continues to live in the home either rent-free or for a nominal monthly sum.
- **Roll-up Loans,** whereby a lump sum is borrowed from a building society, but neither interest nor capital has to be repaid until the house is sold on the death of the owner. These loans can be risky, as the interest owed can mount up very quickly, and it will rarely be appropriate to take such a risk with another person's money.

Whether or not you decide to try to raise income or capital from the value of the home, you must first ensure that the living arrangements of the person you are caring for are secure. This is considered in the section on 'Living arrangements' (p 84). You should also consider the financial implications of selling the home at a later date – for example, if it becomes necessary for the person to move into a private residential or nursing home.

Dealing with taxation

Anyone who has taxable income over a certain level is liable to pay tax, and tax may also be charged when capital is transferred or when someone dies. The way in which taxation affects older people is explained in *Your Taxes and Savings* published each year by Age Concern England. The main points to consider in managing other people's money are summarised here.

Income Tax

Before 6 April 1990, a married couple were treated as one person for Income Tax; the husband had responsibility for paying the tax, most of his wife's income being counted with his own and taxed as joint income. Since that date, however, a system of independent taxation has been introduced, so that married men and women can now be taxed separately.

Married women are now taxpayers in their own right and are responsible for their own tax affairs. You will need to take this into account if you are acting on behalf of one or both of a married couple, as it may be desirable to try to equalise the incomes of husband and wife in order to make full use of their tax allowances.

How is Income Tax worked out?

The Inland Revenue adds up all sources of taxable income and then deducts certain allowances according to the person's circumstances. Income Tax must be paid on the amount that is left, mostly at the lower or basic rate, or at a higher rate for people on a high income. A lower rate of tax has also been introduced for income from savings.

Taxable and non-taxable income

The Table overleaf lists the main kinds of income that older people may receive, according to whether they are taxable or not.

There are many other types of income and benefits, both taxable and non-taxable. Those listed in the Table are the ones that older people are most likely to receive. Further information can be obtained in the free leaflet provided by the Inland Revenue, *Income Tax and Pensioners* (IR 121).

Tax allowances

Everyone is entitled to some kind of tax allowance, which reduces the amount of income on which tax is paid. The levels of tax allowances are normally increased on 6 April each year, usually by an amount at least in line with the rise in prices in the previous calendar year. The main allowances available to older people are outlined below.

Taxable	**Non-taxable**
Earnings	Income Support
Occupational and personal pensions	Housing Benefit
Retirement Pension	Council Tax Benefit
Incapacity Benefit (after 28 weeks)	Incapacity Benefit (first 28 weeks)
Over-80s Pension	Attendance Allowance
Invalid Care Allowance	Disability Living Allowance
Industrial Death Benefit (payable if widowed before 11.4.88)	Disablement Benefit (for industrial injuries)
	Severe Disablement Allowance
Widow's Pension	War Widow's Pension and Allowances
Widowed Mother's Allowance	War Disablement Benefit
Income from most savings accounts and investments	Income from some National Savings investments
Dividends on shares	Gifts and prizes (including National Lottery)
Income from unit trusts	Christmas Bonus
Most income from property	

Personal Allowance

Everyone is entitled to a Personal Allowance, whether married, single, separated, divorced or widowed. There are three different levels of allowance, depending on the person's age during the tax year:

- a basic amount for people under 65;
- a higher amount for those aged between 65 and 74;
- the highest amount for those aged 75 and over.

Married Couple's Allowance

This allowance is available for married couples who live together. It is normally given to the husband, although it can be transferred to the wife or split between them. Again, there are three rates of married couple's allowance: a basic rate for those under 65, a higher amount for those aged 65–74, and the highest amount for those aged 75 and over. The higher allowances are available if *either* partner is or becomes 65 or 75 during the tax year.

If the husband is on a low income and cannot use all or part of the Married Couple's Allowance, the unused part can be transferred to his wife, by writing to his tax office.

Until April 1995 the Married Couples Allowance was all tax-free income. Since then, however, it (and other allowances paid at the same level as the basic Married Couple's Allowance) has been restricted to 15 per cent tax relief. This means that the reduction in a couple's tax bill is now restricted to a maximum of 15 per cent of the value of the allowance, regardless of the rate at which the person receiving the allowance pays tax.

The higher amounts of Personal Allowance and Married Couple's Allowance for those aged 65 and over are reduced when income is over a certain level, but it may be possible to take steps to avoid this.

Widow's Bereavement Allowance

This allowance is available to a widow during the year of her husband's death and the following tax year, if she has not remarried by the start of that year. Again, this provides only 15 per cent tax relief.

Blind Person's Allowance

The Blind Person's Allowance can be claimed by anyone who is registered as blind with the local authority at any time during the tax year.

Claiming for previous years

If the person whose money you are managing has overlooked claiming any of the above allowances in previous years, it may be possible to claim back for six years, if you can prove to the tax office when the person first became entitled to the allowance. This will be paid in the form of a rebate for over-paid tax.

How is Income Tax paid?

People above pension age pay tax in the same way as other tax payers. Those whose only taxable income is their state retirement pension will probably not have to pay tax, as their income will normally be lower than their Personal Allowance. Those who receive an occupational pension or earnings from an employer will be taxed under the PAYE scheme, whereby the employer is told by the tax office how much tax is due, and this is deducted at source before payment of the pension or earnings.

People not covered by the PAYE scheme and those who have other forms of income in addition to their pensions or earnings will be taxed under the self-assessment scheme. This means that they may be sent a tax return form in early April, asking for details of all taxable income received during the previous tax year. If the form is returned before 30 September, the tax office will calculate the amount of tax due and will then send a notice of assessment, which is in effect the tax bill. Those who wish to calculate their own tax have until 31 January to complete and send in the tax return, but there are fixed penalties for late returns. Further information is given in the Inland Revenue leaflet *Self Assessment: a General Guide* (SA/BK1).

Tax returns

If you are responsible for completing someone else's tax return, you must remember to include all sources of income and all investments, with the exception of National Savings Certificates and Premium Bonds (see p 75). You must also be sure to keep records of the person's income and capital gains to be able to complete the tax return the following year.

Capital Gains Tax

If you are involved in selling property, investments or other valuable goods on behalf of another person, you must consider whether Capital Gains Tax will have to be paid. It is advisable to seek advice in order to minimise liability to tax.

Capital Gains Tax is payable on profits made from the sale of valuable goods or property, such as antiques or jewellery, stocks and shares, and in some cases a house. Everyone is allowed to make a certain amount of gain in each year, but anything above that amount is taxed as extra income. Capital Gains Tax may also have to be paid on something that is given away, if it has increased substantially in value since it was acquired, whether by purchase, inheritance or gift.

The following property and goods are not subject to Capital Gains Tax, and do not count towards the annual tax-free allowance:

- gifts between husband and wife while living together;
- the person's only or main private residence;
- private motor vehicles;
- British money;
- foreign currency acquired for personal use outside the UK;
- personal belongings, each item worth up to a specified amount;
- proceeds of most life assurance policies;
- most British Government stocks;
- National Savings certificates;
- Personal Equity Plans (PEPs);
- betting winnings;
- Premium Bond and National Lottery prizes;
- gifts to registered charities;
- compensation or damages for personal injuries.

You should bear in mind the following suggestions of possible ways to minimise Capital Gains Tax:

- Keep gains within the annual tax-free allowance.
- Set off any losses and allowable expenses against gains.
- Postpone the sale of some assets until after the end of the tax year on 5 April.
- Belongings worth more than the maximum specified amount can sometimes be divided into smaller units of less value on which the tax would not be payable.
- Married couples are taxed independently on any gains and both are entitled to a separate tax-free allowance. (As Capital Gains Tax is not payable on gifts between husband and wife, their belongings can be rearranged between them to minimise Inheritance Tax (see below) without paying Capital Gains Tax.)

Inheritance Tax

Inheritance Tax is a tax on the estate of a person who has died, and is payable if the value of the estate is more than a certain amount. This amount is generally raised each year, and the amount that applies is the one in force at the date of death, not when the estate is finally settled.

Gifts over a certain value made by a person within seven years before his or her death will be taken into account in assessing the amount of Inheritance Tax payable, except for gifts between husband and wife and gifts to charities and certain other non-profit-making organisations (eg a political party).

Details of how Inheritance Tax must be paid are given on page 118 under 'Practical arrangements to make after a death'.

Managing savings and investments

When you are responsible for looking after other people's financial affairs, you should try to make sure that any savings and investments they may have are safe and, where appropriate, are producing a secure income. You should not take any undue risks by gambling sums of money on less secure investments unless you have been instructed to do so (eg under a power of attorney). In any case, you cannot normally spend capital or transfer investments without permission, either under a power of attorney or with authority from the Court of Protection.

There are numerous savings and investment schemes, each catering for different needs and carrying varying degrees of risk. Again, this book cannot go into detail but can merely list the main points to look out for when you are managing someone else's money. The Age Concern book *Your Taxes and Savings* gives more detailed information and advice about how to save well and invest wisely.

Getting advice

When you are managing someone else's financial affairs, it will usually be best to obtain independent financial advice, unless the affairs are very simple and straightforward. Although advice on money matters can be obtained from many different sources, few can offer independent advice. Solicitors, stockbrokers and independent financial advisers give this, but most banks and building societies can advise only on their own services and products.

As a result of the Financial Services Act 1986, all firms or individuals offering financial advice have to be registered with an official regulatory body in order to provide some protection against incompetent or untrained advisers. These regulation arrangements are about to be changed, so both the current and the proposed schemes are described.

Under the current regulatory scheme, you should check that the company or individual you are seeking advice from either belongs to one of the Self Regulatory Organisations (SROs) or is authorised by a Recognised Professional Body (RPB). The relevant Self Regulatory Organisations are:

- Personal Investment Authority (PIA)
- Investment Managers Regulatory Organisation (IMRO)
- Securities and Futures Authority (SFA).

Solicitors, accountants, actuaries and insurance brokers whose main activity is not investment business may get authorisation to give financial advice from their own Recognised Professional Body (RPB):

- for solicitors, the Law Society;
- for accountants, either the Institute of Chartered Accountants or the Chartered Association of Certified Accountants;
- for actuaries, the Institute of Actuaries;
- for insurance brokers, the Insurance Brokers Registration Council.

The Government intends to change the regulation arrangements and has announced the setting up (probably in late 1999) of the Financial Services Authority (FSA), a single regulator for the full range of financial businesses. The FSA will replace most of the current regulatory bodies.

Some financial advisers will give advice only about the financial schemes and products of one company (eg a life assurance company or unit trust operator). They are called 'tied agents' and may promote only the products of that particular company. Others are independent financial advisers who can advise on a much wider range of products. Some advisers charge a fee whereas others are commission-based, which means that they make their money from commissions paid on products they sell. When you seek advice, make sure it is from a registered financial adviser and that you know if he or she is tied or independent and how he or she is paid. Sometimes it is useful to talk to more than one adviser before making decisions.

If you wish to complain about your financial adviser – for example, because of dishonesty or negligence – you should take this up first with the firm concerned. If you are not satisfied, you can complain to the relevant regulatory organisation (the Recognised Professional Body or, in future, the proposed new Financial Services Authority), which will tell you how to go about making a formal complaint and give you details of the relevant Ombudsman who can investigate your complaint further. The addresses are on pages 132–137.

Savings and investment schemes

Below is a summary of the savings and investment schemes most commonly used by older people. More detailed information is given in *Your Taxes and Savings*, and independent financial advice should be obtained.

If you are dealing with someone else's financial affairs, one of the following arrangements must usually be made to authorise you to use or have access to their savings or investment accounts:

- a third party mandate (see p 10);
- a power of attorney (p 18);
- an enduring power of attorney, if necessary registered with the Public Trust Office (p 25);
- a Receivership Order from the Court of Protection (p 43);
- a Short Order from the Court of Protection (p 52);
- a Direction of the Public Trustee (p 53).

Bank and building society accounts

Most people keep some or all of their savings in bank or building society accounts. These have the advantage of being generally safe, relatively straightforward and, depending on the type of account, easily accessible.

Savings in bank deposit and building society accounts will earn interest at a rate depending on the type of account. At present, interest on these accounts is paid with the lower rate of tax already deducted and paid on the account holder's behalf. People who do not have to pay tax can apply (on Form R85, available from banks, building societies, post offices and tax offices) to have the interest paid to them gross – ie without deduction of tax. If this is not done in advance, an application can be made for a refund of any tax overpaid in the last six years.

Married couples can be taxed separately. If you are acting for one or both partners of a married couple (so long as there is no conflict between them), it is particularly important to check that you make use of both the husband's and the wife's tax allowances to make sure they are not paying tax unnecessarily.

Tax Exempt Special Savings Accounts (TESSAs)

TESSAs are a particular type of savings account in which up to £9,000 can be invested over a five-year period. It is worth comparing the terms offered by different banks and building societies. Provided the savings are left in the account for the five years, the interest earned will be totally tax-free and can be withdrawn each year. If the capital is touched during this period, the tax exemption is lost and the account becomes a normal deposit account. After April 1999, TESSAs will be phased out and replaced by a new tax-efficient Individual Savings Account (ISA) (see p 77).

National Savings

National Savings investments are regarded as some of the safest ways of saving and investing money. They are backed by the Government, so there is virtually no risk of losing money. There are various types of accounts, bonds and certificates offering different rates of interest according to how accessible the money is. For example, savings in an ordinary account are easy to withdraw through the banking services at the post office, but the interest rate is low. The investment account offers a higher rate of interest, but one month's notice must be given for each withdrawal.

For most National Savings investments, the interest is paid gross (without tax deducted) – which is useful for non-taxpayers. A certain amount of interest paid each year on an ordinary account is tax-free. Other national savings investments, such as National Savings Certificates and Premium Bonds pay their interest (or prizes) free of tax altogether and such interest does not have to be counted as income when calculating any reduction in the higher amounts of tax allowances for people over 65 (see p 67).

Government stock (gilts)

British Government stock (or 'gilt-edged securities' or 'gilts') are similar to National Savings in that they are used to fund the State and certain nationalised industries that are guaranteed by the Government.

There are different types of gilts, with varying time limits for repayment and rates of interest payable. How much interest you get depends on the price at which you buy, but the capital value can go up or down.

Stock Exchange investments

There is always a risk in putting money on the stock market, so it will not normally be appropriate to speculate with other people's money in this way. If the person you are acting for has a substantial portfolio of stocks and shares, or if the investments are complicated in any way, it would be advisable to put them in the hands of a stockbroker or other qualified investment manager.

If you are acting as a receiver or in any other way on behalf of a 'patient' of the Court of Protection (see p 41), you can make use of the services of the panel brokers used by the Public Trust Office, unless you or the patient have made other arrangements.

Dividends from shares are paid net of the lower rate of tax. If the person you are caring for does not have to pay any income tax, this tax can be recovered by claiming for it on the tax return or by writing to the tax office. However, this will not be possible after 6 April 1999, as a result of changes in the July 1997 Budget.

Unit trusts

Unit trusts put together all the money paid by investors (called unit holders) and invest the total among a number of stocks and shares. The managers of the trust will then buy and sell stocks and shares as they see fit, while keeping a reserve of money for investors likely to cash in their units.

If you are acting as a receiver, you can make use of the Common Investment Funds, a collection of three unit trusts available only to patients of the Court of Protection:

- the Capital Fund aims to provide capital growth, income being of less importance;
- the High Yield Fund is designed to produce income coupled with, but greater than, capital growth;
- the Gross Income Fund aims to achieve a high tax-free income return for patients who are not liable to pay income tax.

Further details are available from the Public Trust Office (address on p 136).

Personal Equity Plans (PEPs)

Personal Equity Plans are a tax-efficient form of saving, whereby up to £9,000 can be invested each year through an investment plan manager in shares, unit trusts and investment trusts. There are certain restrictions as to the way those investments are made. PEPs are offered by banks, stockbrokers, unit trust groups, insurance companies and building societies. However, there are risks involved, and it is important to seek advice before investing in PEPs, especially as the arrangements will change following the introduction of the new Individual Savings Account (see below).

Individual Savings Accounts (ISAs)

A new tax-efficient Individual Savings Account was announced in the July 1997 Budget. These will be introduced in April 1999 and will replace TESSAs and PEPs. Investments in ISAs will be subject to annual and maximum limits – check with your financial adviser for the relevant criteria.

Help and advice

If you are trying to find the safest form of investment or one that produces the greatest income, or the investments are complicated, it is best to seek advice. Remember to check that you are getting independent advice from a registered financial adviser.

Dealing with expenditure

It is your responsibility to ensure that the needs of the person whose money you are managing are being met. This will include their day-to-day expenses, their maintenance costs and outgoings as well as those of any dependants for whom they should be providing. The following is a checklist of the regular costs that may have to be covered:

- accommodation costs (rent, mortgage repayments, service charges, water charges, repairs and maintenance costs, residential care or nursing home fees, etc);
- Council Tax (unless severely mentally impaired and living alone or main residence is in hospital, residential or nursing home care);
- food and other living expenses;
- clothing;
- household bills (gas, electricity, etc);
- television licence;
- cost of looking after pets;
- insurance (for property, household contents, other valuables, etc);
- life assurance;
- loans and credit agreement payments (bank loans, credit card payments, TV rental costs, etc);
- personal needs (eg tobacco, toiletries, newspapers, books, etc);
- one-off payments to meet particular needs (eg glasses, mobility aids, a particular item of furniture, greetings cards and presents, etc).

You may need to add to this checklist to take account of the particular needs of the person you are acting for.

You should also look to see if the person you are acting for has any debts and, if so, make arrangements for these to be paid off gradually or written off, depending on the circumstances (see p 81).

You will probably be familiar with how to deal with most of the above, as they will generally require the same procedures as managing your own affairs. Some further hints are given below or in references to other sections of the book.

Paying the bills

Standing orders

If the person you are acting for has a bank, post office or building society account that you can use, the best arrangement for paying bills could be by standing order, whereby a pre-arranged amount of money is taken from the account at regular intervals (usually monthly) and paid direct to the creditor.

This method is also helpful for people who find it hard to remember when bills are due for payment. You must be sure to check that there is enough money coming into the account to cover all the standing orders you arrange and that the correct amounts are being paid out. Standing orders are regularly used for mortgage repayments, water rates, Council Tax, etc, and can be used for most regular outgoings.

It is also possible to pay gas and electricity bills by standing order using the monthly budget schemes. Under these schemes, the yearly consumption of fuel is estimated and the cost spread out evenly over the year, so that payment can be made automatically by standing order each month. You should check that the estimates are reasonable to avoid accumulating too much credit in the relevant accounts.

Standing orders can normally be arranged by filling in a form provided by the creditor, but most banks and building societies also supply their own forms. You can cancel a standing order at any time.

Direct debit

Direct debits are similar to standing orders, but are more flexible because both the date and the amount payable can be varied by the recipient. Only organisations authorised by one of the major banks or building societies (eg gas and electricity suppliers, insurance companies) can ask for payment by direct debit. They provide their own forms to be completed and sent to the bank or building society, which then makes the payment.

Creditors must give advance notice of any changes they wish to make in the amount payable or the date of payment. You can cancel a direct debit at any time. If you use this procedure, it is important to monitor the bank account at regular intervals to make sure that the debits are correct and needed, and that there will be sufficient funds in the account to meet them.

Direct payments by the Benefits Agency

If the person you are acting for is receiving Income Support and has debts or arrears to be paid off, it may be possible for certain bills to be paid direct by the Benefits Agency. The Benefits Agency will deduct from the benefit a regular weekly amount towards the bill, together with an amount to pay off the arrears, and pay this direct to the creditor.

Reducing expenditure

In some cases, you may need to reduce the overall level of expenditure if it is regularly higher than the overall level of income. Ensuring that money is spent wisely is the best way to keep expenditure down, but there are also a number of specific ways of reducing expenditure. These are outlined below.

Life assurance

The person whose affairs you have taken over may have a life assurance policy, either as part of an endowment mortgage (see p 86) or separately. You will need to consider:

- whether the policy should be kept up by continuing to pay the premiums;
- whether to change to a different policy with cheaper premiums;
- whether the policy should be converted to a paid-up policy, if this is possible;
- whether the policy should be surrendered for cash.

In order to decide what is most appropriate, particularly if you need money immediately to pay for some necessary expense (eg house repairs), you will have to find out the following information from the insurance company:

- What is the *surrender value* of the policy (the amount the company will pay in cash if you stop paying the premiums and cancel the policy)?
- What is the *paid-up value* of the policy (the amount the company will agree to pay out at the end of the term of the policy or when the policy-holder dies, if you stop paying the premiums now but do not cancel the policy)?
- When is the policy due to mature?

The tax implications must also be considered, particularly for people paying tax at the higher rate. Tax relief is payable on policies taken out before 13 March 1984, but this has been abolished for policies taken out after that date.

If the life assurance policy is part of an endowment mortgage, you should also consider whether the policy can be sold to someone else, rather than surrendered. You will also need to negotiate with the lender to see if it is possible to transfer to a capital repayment mortgage if you decide to surrender or sell all or part of the policy (see p 86).

It would be wise to seek independent financial advice on the best options, and for help in the negotiations.

Changing the type of mortgage

It may be possible to reduce mortgage costs by changing the type of mortgage or altering the repayment terms. This is dealt with in more detail in the next section on 'Living Arrangements' (p 84).

Paying off loans or credit agreements

Loans from banks and finance companies can place a heavy burden on regular expenditure. In some instances it might be better to pay these off, especially if there is available capital but income is fairly restricted.

Hire purchase agreements and conditional sale agreements can involve repossession of goods if arrears build up. You must be particularly careful with these types of loan, as you may end up having to pay all the arrears as well as losing the goods. However, hire purchase and conditional sale agreements are rare these days.

Dealing with debts

When you take over managing another person's money, you may find that they have previously built up debts that will need sorting out. If you are having to deal with excessive or complicated debts, it is best to seek advice. Many Citizens Advice Bureaux have considerable experience in dealing with debt problems. Help may also be obtained from other advice agencies and from some solicitors.

If you are acting on behalf of someone who is mentally incapacitated, it is important to consider whether any debts are actually 'enforceable'.

Debts can only be enforced if the debtor and creditor have made a valid contract, which will normally be the case if both parties understood what they were doing at the time, even if the debtor no longer does.

However, if the debtor was mentally incapacitated to the extent that he or she did not understand the transaction that led to the debt and the creditor was aware of the incapacity, there is no binding contract between them and the debt cannot be enforced. The only exception to this is if the contract was for 'necessaries', which means goods that are necessary for life and for the person's actual requirements at the time of the sale, in which case it can be enforced.

The following checklist may help you to deal with any debts, particularly if there are several.

- Check that the person you are acting for really does owe the money:
  - was there a valid contract?
  - is someone else liable?
  - is the amount correct?
- Contact the creditors and explain the situation:
  - they are more likely to be helpful and understanding if you contact them before they start chasing the debt.
- Collect details of all the debts:
  - you need to know exactly what debts you are dealing with and whether the person you are acting for has taken any steps to repay them.
- Find out what action the creditor is taking to recover the debt:
  - have legal proceedings been started?
  - some creditors may decide it is not worthwhile trying to recover the debt.
- Work out the priority order for dealing with the debts:
  - some debts have more dire consequences (eg eviction for rent arrears), and this is a vital factor in determining priorities;
  - debts that affect the person's essential living expenditure or basic circumstances are always a priority;
  - if legal proceedings have been started, this may affect the order of priority.

- Find out whether the debts can be paid off:
  - has income been maximised (eg by claiming benefits or tax rebates)?
  - is there any surplus income?
  - can any lump sums be raised (eg from charities, help from relatives, or by surrendering life assurance)?
- Work out repayment proposals:
  - payments for priority debts must be worked out before other debts;
  - it may be possible to offer repayment over a period of time;
  - offer only what can be afforded;
  - if offering deferred payments, make sure that any interest payments will not be increased.
- Keep up regular repayments:
  - if you cannot pay, or if circumstances change, always tell the creditor and explain why.

Administration Orders

In some circumstances it may be advantageous to apply to the Court for an Administration Order. This is possible when someone has a County Court judgment against them for one or more debts, totalling £5,000 or less. The effect of such an Order is that the Court will notify all creditors and will make arrangements for payment, either in full or by instalment. Seek advice from a money adviser about this.

Further information

Details of some useful publications containing information on the issues mentioned in this section are given on pages 139–140. Further help and advice can be obtained from the organisations listed on pages 130–137.

Living Arrangements

Managing other people's money also often involves looking after their living arrangements. You may have to manage a property or make sure that rent or fees are paid for other accommodation. In taking over other people's affairs, you should consider what needs to be done, either to secure their present living arrangements or to arrange a move to more suitable accommodation. You have no power to dictate where the person should live, but in practice, if you control the finances, you may find yourself 'in charge'.

When the person you are acting for is able to express a view, it is important that you take his or her wishes into account and do not force changes that are not acceptable or not necessary. When the person is not able to make a decision, unless you are acting under a registered enduring power of attorney (see p 27), it will usually be necessary to involve and obtain the approval of the Court of Protection or the Public Trustee (see p 41) before any major changes can be made in living arrangements.

You should remember that, when you are looking after someone else's financial affairs, it is your responsibility to protect the interests of the person you are acting for. You must ensure that proper arrangements are made, not only for present accommodation needs but also to provide for possible changes in circumstances in the future (eg if the person later requires a greater degree of care).

The law relating to housing and property rights is complicated, so it may often be necessary for you to seek legal advice.

The main points you should consider in relation to living arrangements are outlined in the following pages. Various housing options are discussed – staying put, sharing a home, moving into retirement housing or residential care, as well as temporary periods away from home, either for respite care or going into hospital. Most of these issues are considered in greater detail in various factsheets published by Age Concern England (see pp 141–142).

Staying put

For someone who is living at home, and is likely to continue to do so, you will need to:

- make sure that payment of the rent or the mortgage is kept up;
- make sure that any necessary insurance policies are maintained (property and contents);
- consider whether help is required to support the person at home;
- make sure that any necessary repairs are carried out;
- consider whether any improvements or adaptations are required.

Paying the rent

If there is any difficulty in paying the rent, you should check to see that the person you are acting for is receiving all the income he or she is entitled to. This might include claiming Social Security benefits or help from the local authority, in particular Housing Benefit and Council Tax Benefit (see p 63). You might also see if it is possible to re-invest any savings to produce income, and check that the person is not paying tax unnecessarily (see pp 72–77).

You should also contact the landlord to explain the position and make arrangements to pay off any rent arrears gradually (see 'Dealing with debts' on p 81).

If the person you are acting for is in privately rented accommodation, you should check to make sure the rent has not been set too high and, if it has, whether there is any chance of getting it reduced. You must first find out what sort of tenancy it is. You will need to seek advice about this from an advice agency or solicitor, as it can be complicated.

If the tenancy started before 15 January 1989 and it is a **regulated** or **protected** tenancy, you should be able to apply to the Rent Officer at the local council to fix a 'fair rent'.

If the tenancy started after 15 January 1989 and it is an **assured** tenancy or an **assured shorthold** tenancy, you may be able to apply to the Rent Assessment Committee to fix a **market rent**, which is the maximum that can be charged. However, there is a risk that the Rent Assessment Committee might fix the rent at a higher level than the landlord is charging.

If the tenancy is an **assured fixed-term** tenancy, the landlord can charge whatever amount the tenant agreed to pay (but no more) for the fixed term. If the landlord tries to put up the rent at the end of that period, you can apply to the Rent Assessment Committee to fix a market rent.

All tenancies that started on or after 28 February 1997 will automatically be an **assured shorthold** tenancy, unless they specifically say otherwise. For these tenancies, an application may only be made to the Rent Assessment Committee once within six months of the beginning of the tenancy.

Further information about private tenancies and rents is given in Age Concern Factsheet 36, *Private tenants' rights*.

Paying the mortgage

If there are difficulties paying the mortgage, again it is important to check that the person you are acting for is receiving the full entitlement to income. You should contact the lender to explain the position and make arrangements to pay off any mortgage arrears gradually.

It may also be possible to change the mortgage repayments to cut the costs. This will depend on what type of mortgage it is and whether the lender will agree to any changes. However, if an older person has been paying off a mortgage for many years, you will need to take into account the fact that there may be only a few years left when working out ways of dealing with payment problems.

There are three main types of mortgage, described below.

Repayment mortgages whereby the monthly repayments are made up of interest on the amount borrowed plus an amount towards repaying the capital of the loan, which will be paid off gradually over the term of the mortgage. Repayment mortgages do not give life assurance cover, but some mortgagees may have bought a 'mortgage protection policy', which pays off the mortgage if the owner dies. These policies do not, however, give life assurance cover beyond the end of the mortgage and the premiums may be very expensive, particularly for an older person.

Endowment mortgages whereby interest only is paid to the lender and an 'endowment premium' is paid to a life assurance company. The endowment policy matures either at the end of the mortgage term or on the death of the owner. A 'full' endowment mortgage is intended to clear the mortgage debt and may provide extra capital on maturity. A 'low cost' endowment mortgage is intended to pay off the mortgage capital loan in one lump sum, but there have been instances in which the final sum was not sufficient to cover the mortgage debt.

Interest-only mortgages whereby only interest is paid to the lender and no endowment policy is involved. The capital is repaid by the sale of the property on the death of the owner or earlier.

There are a variety of other mortgage arrangements available, including a combination of the different types of mortgage. It would be wise to seek proper independent financial advice before making any changes, in particular to discuss ways of reducing repayment costs.

Reducing repayment costs

The lender may agree to accept 'interest-only' payments, at least for a while, if you can explain that there are immediate financial problems that are likely to improve. This may be helpful for people on Income Support (see p 62), because they may be able to get benefit towards some or all of the mortgage interest as part of their housing costs, but not the capital repayments.

Another possibility is to ask the lender to extend the term of the mortgage, which will reduce the monthly payments. However, the lender is unlikely to agree to this if the owner is already quite old.

Personal support and community care services

People who live in their own homes may need some support to enable them to continue to care for themselves. The following are suggestions of some of the support services that may be provided by the local authority, health authority, private agency or voluntary organisation.

- home help/home care workers;
- meals-on-wheels;
- district nursing care;
- help with baths, etc, at home;
- aids and adaptations;

- visiting schemes;
- attendance at day centres and clubs;
- provision of a telephone;
- laundry facilities;
- alarm call system;
- breaks and holidays away from home;
- use of volunteers for decorating, gardening, etc.

In the first instance, you should contact the local authority social services department and ask them to carry out a community care assessment of the person you are acting for. The local authority has a duty under the NHS and Community Care Act 1990 to assess anyone who seems to be in need of community care or other support services. Further details of the assessment procedure can be found on Age Concern Factsheet 41, *Local authority assessments for community care services*. If the person is being looked after by an informal carer, such as a family member or friend, the carer can also request – under the Carers (Recognition and Services) Act 1995 – that their ability to provide, and to continue to provide, care is assessed at the same time.

The availability of the services listed above varies greatly between different areas. The local authority will decide what kind of help, if any, it can offer; it could be provided direct by the social services department or they could arrange for services to be provided by a charity or private agency. If a health or housing need is identified during the assessment, the local authority must contact the relevant department to see if the necessary services can be arranged. If you or the person you are acting for don't agree with the assessment or with the services offered, you can make a complaint through the social services complaints procedure, or seek legal advice to see if the decision can be challenged.

Local authorities can charge for the services they arrange, and the amount will depend on the financial circumstances of the person receiving the services. It may in some cases be possible (and cheaper) to purchase the above services privately, without the involvement of the local authority. If funds are available, consideration could be given to the employment of a housekeeper or gardener or other domestic help. Further information is given in Age Concern Factsheet 6, *Finding help at home*.

Repairs and improvements

Responsibility for repairs will depend on whether the accommodation is rented or owner-occupied.

In *rented accommodation*, the landlord is responsible for the structure, exterior and installations (eg plumbing, electric wiring) of the property and for all major repairs, while the tenant will usually be responsible for internal and minor repairs, depending on the tenancy agreement. Further details are available in Age Concern Factsheet 35, *Rights for council and housing association tenants*, and Factsheet 36, *Private tenants' rights*.

It is not advisable to withhold the rent to try to force the landlord to carry out repairs, because this could result in losing the tenancy. If you are having problems in getting repairs done or have other problems concerning the condition of the property, it is best to seek help from an advice agency or a solicitor experienced in this type of work. For private tenants, the environmental health department of your local council may also be able to help.

Some private tenants, particularly those who are elderly, ill or frail, and those in receipt of Income Support, Housing Benefit or Council Tax Benefit, may be able to get a home repair assistance grant from the local authority if they are responsible for repairs under the terms of their tenancy agreement (see p 90).

Owner-occupiers are generally responsible for carrying out their own repairs, although, for leasehold properties, the freeholder may have some responsibility for external or structural repairs. If the person you are acting for does not have money available for repairs, you should investigate the possibility of getting a loan or a grant. It is worth trying the following sources.

Social Fund grants and loans

People who are receiving Income Support may be able to claim a loan or a grant from the Social Fund (see p 63) as follows.

Budgeting Loans are discretionary, but some priority is given to applications for essential home repairs and maintenance when a bank loan or mortgage is not available, or if refusal could result in hardship or damage to the home or risk to the health or safety of a member of the household. A loan will be given only if you can show that it can be repaid.

Community Care Grants are discretionary grants, available to help people to stay in their own homes, and are not repayable. They are directed at 'priority groups', which include people with mental or physical disability or illness or general frailty.

Crisis Loans are for emergency needs only (eg after a fire or flood) and will be given only if they can be repaid.

Local authority grants

People on a low income who are living in a property that requires repair or adaptation may qualify for one of the following discretionary, means-tested, grants from the local authority.

Renovation Grants for larger repairs and improvements or conversion work. Priority may be given to properties that are 'unfit for human habitation' or in serious disrepair, or that require insulation or more adequate heating. The owner must have lived in the property for at least three years.

Home repair assistance for 'elderly, disabled or infirm' and some other low income occupiers, to pay for minor but essential repairs, improvements or adaptations up to a specified amount, although more than one application can be made.

Help with adaptations

Some help may be available from the local authority towards the cost of adaptations required by people with disabilities who are on a low income. The **Disabled Facilities Grant** is mandatory for disabled people who qualify financially and have difficulties with access to their own homes or to the basic amenities within it. Discretionary grants may also be available for other adaptations to make a home suitable for a disabled person.

Building alterations are subject to value-added tax (VAT), but certain alterations for people with disabilities are zero-rated; that is, no VAT is payable for such things as constructing ramps, widening doors, installing alarm systems and putting in hand rails.

Further details of the help available towards the cost of repairs, improvements and adaptations are available in Age Concern Factsheet 13, *Older home owners: financial help with repairs and adaptations*.

Other sources of finance

It may be possible to borrow money from a bank, building society or reputable finance company, either by raising an extra loan on top of an existing mortgage or by taking out a separate loan. For people receiving Income Support, the Benefits Agency will normally increase the weekly amount to cover some or all the interest payable on a loan for major repairs that are necessary to maintain the fabric of the property or for essential improvements (eg damp-proofing, insulation, improving ventilation).

Sharing a home

Most people have lived in a shared home at some time in their lives, usually with a spouse or partner, or with relatives or friends. Few people will have considered the legal implications of sharing a home, as, if the arrangement works out well, the legal consequences are usually not important.

Sharing a home is a possibility often considered by older people, either moving in with a son or daughter to live communally or in a 'granny flat', or by a younger person moving in with a parent or older relative.

Such arrangements can work out well, as it may be a means of providing older people with the care and support they need. However, it is essential to have clear and legally enforceable agreements between the people concerned about rights to live in the home, meeting the costs involved, what happens if one person wishes to leave, or dies, etc.

Housing rights in a shared home depend on a number of factors:

- the type of accommodation (rented or owner-occupied);
- who shares the accommodation;
- whether they are or have been married to each other;
- what agreement was made when they first moved in together or later.

Married people

If the people who share the home are married to each other, they will normally have equal rights over the property, regardless of whether the property is in joint names. This means that both have the right to stay in the property, and either can pay the rent or mortgage.

Unmarried people

The situation is far more complicated for people sharing a home who are not married. Some 'cohabiting' couples may have a formal agreement setting out their respective rights, but between members of a family or between friends, there is a common and natural reluctance to make formal legal agreements. However, without such agreements, it becomes very difficult to sort things out if the arrangement breaks down.

Different generations

In the case of an older person sharing a home with younger relatives, particular care must be taken to ensure that agreement is reached, not only about the arrangement itself – which parts of the property the older person can use for him- or herself, etc – but also what will happen if things don't work out.

Relationships can all too easily break down, or something may happen to a member of the household that means the shared house must be sold, for example because of a death, divorce, redundancy or the need to move for employment reasons. Or the older person may later need a greater degree of care than others in the house can give.

It is therefore important that you seek legal advice on behalf of the person you are acting for, before such an arrangement is entered into. The main points to note are:

- If the person is not contributing any capital to the shared home, his or her rights to stay in the home must be clarified.
- If capital is to be provided, either to pay for an extension to the property or in order to purchase a larger property for them all to occupy, it must be clarified whether this is a gift or a loan, and how the capital will be calculated and could be recovered if things go wrong or if it were needed to pay for residential care.

- It is also important to establish who owns what share of the property, because, if one of the co-owners dies, a proportion of the property may form part of the estate.

Moving into retirement housing or sheltered accommodation

Few people enjoy the disruption of moving unless they are going to somewhere that they will feel more comfortable. Many people will not want to move unless it is absolutely necessary. For people who have no relatives to move in with but who need someone at hand to help out when they need it, a move into retirement housing (also known as sheltered accommodation) may be the best arrangement. For others who need a greater degree of care, it may be necessary to consider a move into residential care. It is important to consider what help might be required, both now and in the future, to reduce the likelihood of having to move again.

Retirement housing usually consists of self-contained flats or bungalows in a purpose-built complex with communal facilities, such as lounges, laundry facilities, gardens and a guest room for visitors. There is normally a resident manager or warden who generally acts as a 'good neighbour' and can call for help in an emergency, but cannot provide help with shopping, cooking, dressing or nursing care. Each unit should have an alarm call system and should be properly equipped for older people – for example, with hand rails and ramps, and everything placed within easy reach.

Some schemes, known as 'very sheltered housing' or 'extra-care sheltered housing', provide a higher level of care with additional services such as meals and cleaning. Although such schemes have a higher staffing level to help with the personal care of residents, nursing care is not generally provided.

Retirement housing can be either rented or owner-occupied. The Elderly Accommodation Council (address on p 134) provides a list of retirement housing schemes for sale or rent.

Buying retirement housing

If you are considering buying retirement housing on behalf of another person, you must take into account the expenses involved. Retirement housing is not cheap to buy, although, as well as newly built properties, an increasing number of resales are becoming available. There will also be service charges to pay to cover the warden's salary, the upkeep of the premises, water charges, heat, light and power for the communal areas, and for any other facilities that may be provided.

It is also important to get legal advice to check the terms of the deeds (with a flat, this will usually be a lease). Also, check that the builders of newly built properties are members of the National House Building Council (NHBC) and are abiding by the terms of the NHBC's *Code of Practice for Sheltered Housing*. The management organisation should also be a member of the Association of Retirement Housing Managers (ARHM), which has its own Code of Practice. Further information is provided in Age Concern Factsheet 2, *Retirement housing for sale*.

Retirement housing to rent

Retirement or sheltered housing to rent is generally provided by local authorities and some housing associations. Waiting lists are normally long, and each authority or housing association has its own allocations policy, taking into account people's physical and social needs.

The Abbeyfield Society provides a particular sort of supportive sheltered accommodation for people looking for companionship. The accommodation is purpose-built or in houses converted into unfurnished bed-sitting rooms with a communal dining room, where main meals are provided by the resident housekeeper.

In rented retirement housing, service charges are payable as well as or included in the rent. Help with these costs may be available through Housing Benefit for those who are eligible, but this may change in the future. Check with Age Concern or a local advice agency.

Temporary periods away from home

The person whose affairs you are looking after may need to go away from home for temporary periods, for example into hospital for treatment or for a respite stay in residential care. You might have to make arrangements for the home to be looked after during that time and to sort out the person's entitlement to benefits or other income.

Respite care

Some local and health authorities make provision for temporary respite care in their own residential homes and hospitals, or they can arrange for temporary care to be provided by a charity or private organisation. You may also be able to make your own arrangements for respite care in a private or voluntary home if funds are available.

In the first instance, you should ask the local authority social services to carry out a community care assessment of the person concerned (see p 88), to find out what services are needed, including respite care. Help with paying for respite care will be similar to that provided for residential or nursing care (see p 99), except that the value of the home will not be taken into account.

Going into hospital

The main effect that going into hospital has on a person's finances is that most Social Security benefits will be reduced after the patient has been in hospital for four or six weeks. There is then a further reduction in benefit after one year in hospital. This does not apply to all benefits, and the amount of the reduction differs according to the different types of benefit.

If the person you are acting for goes into hospital, you should tell the Benefits Agency immediately, if he or she receives any benefits. You should also check that all relevant benefits are being claimed and that you can receive payments of benefits on behalf of the person in hospital (see p 33).

Patients who are incapable of managing money

Hospital authorities have the right to reduce the amount of money a patient receives at any one time, if the doctor responsible for the patient's care decides that:

- the patient's mental or physical condition makes him or her unable to handle more than a limited amount of cash or any at all; *or*

- it is necessary on therapeutic grounds to restrict the amount of cash that the patient should handle while in hospital.

If this happens to the person you are acting for, you should contact the doctor and explain how you are using the patient's money on his or her behalf, and what needs the patient has to continue to receive payments.

When the time comes for the person you are acting for to be discharged from hospital, you may need to be involved in making arrangements for them to receive continuing health care services from the NHS or support services from the local authority. You should be kept fully informed by the hospital and by social services staff of the procedures for hospital discharge and how any assessment for services will work. Further information is given in Age Concern Factsheet 37, *Hospital discharge arrangements and NHS continuing health care services*.

Convalescent and respite health care

Health authorities and GP fundholders also make arrangements to provide and fund respite health care, in particular for people who have complex health care needs requiring medical or nursing supervision, or those who are receiving a package of health care in their own homes and they or their carer needs a break. When the NHS makes these arrangements, there is no charge to the patient. The health authority must publish its criteria for respite health care.

Local authorities also set criteria for respite care, and can arrange or provide this as part of a package of care for the person or to help support a carer. Either way, if the local authority arranges or provides respite care, there may be a charge to pay. Age Concern Factsheet 37, *Hospital discharge arrangements and NHS continuing health care services*, and Factsheet 41, *Local authority assessments for community care services*, may be helpful.

Protection of furniture and other belongings

While the person you are acting for is in hospital or respite care and likely to be away from home for some weeks, you will normally need to make arrangements to ensure that furniture and other belongings are protected. If the property is left empty, you should check with the insurance company that the property and its contents will still be covered. If not, you may need to arrange alternative insurance cover or remove belongings to a safe place.

Some people may have to be admitted urgently to hospital or local authority residential care, because of accident or sudden illness, or because they need looking after or have been removed from home against their will and compulsorily admitted. In these circumstances, the local social services authority has a duty to protect 'any moveable property' left in the person's home if there is no one else to do it. This could include making arrangements for a pet to be looked after, as well as protecting household contents.

If there is a risk of loss of, or damage to, any of the person's belongings and no suitable arrangements have been made to protect them, the local authority has the right to go into the home and take any necessary steps to 'prevent or mitigate' the loss or damage, and can charge the person, or anyone responsible for the person's money, for any expenses incurred.

Residential and nursing home care

A move into residential care is a very serious decision, particularly if you are involved in making that decision on someone else's behalf, even if only from the financial point of view. The considerations that you must take into account, both in deciding whether admission into a residential or nursing home is appropriate and in choosing a suitable home, are detailed in Age Concern Factsheet 29, *Finding residential and nursing home accommodation*.

Preparing for admission into residential care

Having decided that a move into a residential or nursing home is appropriate, there are a number of further decisions to be made and matters to be sorted out. These include:

- the choice of residential or nursing home;
- what the costs are and how to pay for them;
- what happens to the current home;
- what happens to furniture and other belongings.

Choosing a residential home

Residential homes provide board and personal care. One of the first considerations in choosing a residential home is where in the country this should be. For example, is it important for the person to stay in the area where he or she has recently lived, and so remain close to friends and familiar surroundings, or is it more appropriate to move to be near relatives or back to the person's place of origin? You should think this through carefully if you are making the decision on someone else's behalf.

The next decision is about the type of residential care. Residential homes can be owned and run by private individuals or companies, by charitable or voluntary sector organisations, or by the local authority. Local authority residential homes are sometimes known as 'Part III' · homes, after the legislation (Part III of the National Assistance Act 1948) that allows local authorities to provide this type of care.

Private and voluntary sector residential homes that cater for four or more residents must, by law, be registered with the local authority, which ensures that they meet certain standards. The local authority must inspect the homes at least twice a year, and must make copies of their inspection reports available to the public – although in practice this may mean visiting the local authority's Inspection and Registration Unit's offices during working hours. Private and voluntary sector homes that cater for fewer than four residents must also be registered, but under a simpler procedure. At present, local authority 'Part III' homes are not required by law to be registered, although they must be inspected. The Government has announced plans to change this system of registration, but this is unlikely to happen before the year 2000.

Choosing a nursing home

Nursing homes provide nursing care by qualified nurses for people who are ill or infirm. It is the presence of qualified nurses that distinguishes nursing home care from residential home care. Most nursing homes are run privately, but some are provided by voluntary agencies and charities. All private and voluntary sector nursing homes must be registered with the health authority's Inspection and Registration Unit, and must be inspected twice a year. With effect from the summer of

1998, a requirement has been placed on health authorities to make their inspection reports public.

The NHS provides a small number of nursing homes but these do not have to be registered or inspected. In some cases the health authority may purchase a place in a voluntary or private sector nursing home for a patient who has continuing health care needs, as an alternative to a long-stay ward in hospital. In such instances there will be no charge to the patient and the costs are met by the NHS. However, most older people living in private or voluntary sector nursing homes do not meet the criteria for continuing NHS care and so must pay towards this care from their own income and savings (see below to p 104). Further details are contained in Age Concern Factsheet 37, *Hospital discharge arrangements and NHS continuing health care services.*

Dual registered homes

Some homes are dual registered – that is, they are registered with both the local authority and the health authority to provide residential and nursing home levels of care. In such homes a resident might not have to move to a different home if they eventually need more, or less, care.

Homes for very disabled or mentally frail people

It may be difficult to find a home for someone who is very frail, either mentally or physically, particularly if he or she is too frail for a residential home but not ill enough to require nursing home care. It is advisable to seek help from the family doctor and to ask for an assessment of the person's care needs from the local authority social services department. One of the specialist organisations listed on pages 130–137 may be able to offer advice.

Paying for residential and nursing home care

A priority concern in choosing a residential or nursing home is that, so far as possible, it should be a home for life. Obviously, it may not be possible to foresee an illness or frailty that requires a move into another home or into hospital. But what should be avoided is the need to move for financial reasons, for example if funds to pay for private care run out. This will require careful planning, as there is no doubt that admission to residential care will lead to a reduction in the resident's resources.

The financial help available depends on the type of residential or nursing home and the date of entering into residential or nursing home care. A brief outline of the main provisions is given here. Further details can be found in the book *Your Rights* and in the latest factsheets published by Age Concern England. The position is extremely complicated and a number of cases have been taken to court, which have affected the legal position. You are therefore advised to seek specialist advice from a solicitor or from one of the organisations listed on pages 130–137 if admission to residential or nursing home care seems to be a possibility, either now or in the future

If no financial help is required

If the person you are acting for has sufficient funds to be able to pay the full costs of care, both now and in the future, you can make your own arrangements for admission into a residential or nursing home run by a private or voluntary organisation, which will include arrangements for paying the fees. There may be no need to involve the local authority, but even though financial help may not be required, it might be useful to ask the local authority social services to carry out an assessment of the person's needs (see p 88) to help you decide which type of home would be most suitable.

If the person is receiving Attendance Allowance (see p 61), this will continue to be payable after admission into a private or voluntary sector home. However, it will be withdrawn after four weeks if the residential care was arranged and funded by the local authority or if the person is living in a local authority home.

If financial help is required

If the person you are acting for is likely to need financial assistance to pay residential or nursing home fees, either immediately or in the future, you should ask the local authority to carry out an assessment of the person's needs as soon as admission to residential care becomes a possibility (see p 88). After the assessment, the local authority will decide what help, if any, they can offer, to provide either services in the person's own home or a place in a residential or nursing home.

Each local authority will have different criteria for making these decisions. If you don't agree with the assessment or with the help offered, you can make a complaint through the social services complaints procedure, or seek legal advice to see if the decision can be challenged. (See Age Concern Factsheet 41, *Local authority assessments for community care services*, for more information.)

If the local authority decides that residential or nursing home care is needed, it will offer a place and set a standard weekly rate, which is the amount it will cost the authority to provide a suitable place to meet the person's assessed needs. If the person cannot afford to pay the standard rate, the local authority will carry out a means test to assess the contribution the resident can afford to pay.

If you or the person you are acting for prefers to choose a different home, the local authority should agree to this so long as your chosen home will meet the resident's assessed needs. However, if the fees are more expensive than the standard rate, you will have to make your own arrangements to pay the difference – for example, by asking for contributions from relatives, friends or a charity. Age Concern Factsheet 10, *Local authority charging procedures for residential and nursing home care*, explains the rules in detail.

Private and voluntary homes

If the local authority arranges a place in a home run by a private or voluntary organisation, the authority will be responsible for paying the full fees to the home. If the resident has been asked to pay a contribution, arrangements can be made for these to be paid either to the local authority or directly to the home.

Residents in private or voluntary homes may still be able to claim Income Support, if they qualify financially, which will include a 'residential allowance' towards the care fees. Any entitlement to Income Support will be taken into account in assessing the resident's contribution, but all residents must be left with a weekly allowance to cover personal expenses, the level of which is set by Parliament.

Local authority homes

Residents in local-authority-run homes may also have to pay a contribution towards the fees, assessed in the same way as for residents placed in private or voluntary homes. However, they will not normally be able to claim Income Support unless their income is below the level of the basic state Retirement Pension. Again, all residents must be left with a small weekly allowance for personal expenses.

People in residential or nursing home care before 1 April 1993

A different funding system exists for people who were already in a private or voluntary home (but not a local authority home) before 1 April 1993. Such residents are covered by 'preserved rights' to special higher levels of Income Support to help pay the fees, so long as they qualify financially. The levels are set by Parliament, according to different categories of age and disability of the residents. Details of this scheme are set out in Age Concern Factsheet 11, *Financial support for people in residential and nursing homes prior to 1 April 1993.*

Moving to a different residential care home

Special arrangements may be necessary for people wishing to move to another local authority area, or who wish to move to a more expensive residential care place than the local authority is willing to arrange. They will usually have to get relatives, friends or charities to help with 'top-up' payments.

What happens to the person's own home?

If you are managing the affairs of someone who goes into residential care, it is likely that you will have to sort out what happens to the current home. This will depend on a number of factors:

- whether the home is rented or owned;
- whether it is in sole or joint names;
- whether anyone else lives there;
- whether the value of the property will be taken into account in funding the residential care place;
- whether anyone else has a right of 'succession' to the tenancy – ie to take over the tenancy when the tenant dies;
- whether the person whose home it is has left the property to someone in his or her Will.

If no help is required to pay residential care fees

If the home is in joint names, or if someone else has a right to the property, you may only have to ensure that proper arrangements are made for the management of the property to be taken over by that person.

In other circumstances there may be someone who is willing to take on the responsibility of looking after the house. This could be because they expect to gain the right to own or live in it when the person dies, possibly because they are named in the Will as beneficiary or for other reasons. In making such an arrangement, however, care must be taken to ensure that the interests of the owner (or tenant) are properly safeguarded. Property rights are extremely complicated, so it would be best for you to ask for legal advice to establish these.

If no one else is entitled to the property, you may have to make arrangements for it to be sold or for the tenancy to be terminated. You can do this only if you have been given authority under a power of attorney (see p 18) or have permission from the Court of Protection or the Public Trustee (see p 41).

If help is required to pay residential care fees

Residents whose care has been arranged by the local authority and who own their own homes cannot be forced to sell property to pay for their care. However, the value of the property may be taken into account in assessing the resident's contribution towards care fees (except in some cases where close relatives continue to live there; see below). The local authority can also take steps to recover unpaid contributions, or it can place a legal charge on the value of the property, so that it can recover the money owed whenever the property is sold.

The value of the home must be disregarded if it continues to be occupied by one or more of the following:

- the resident's married partner or former cohabitee;
- a close relative who is 60 or over;
- a relative under 60 who is disabled;
- a child under 16 whom the resident is liable to maintain.

If the home is jointly owned, the resident's share will be taken into account unless the above exceptions apply. The local authority also has a discretionary power to ignore the value of the home in other circumstances if hardship would be caused. Further information is given in Age Concern Factsheet 38, *Treatment of the former home as capital for people in residential and nursing homes.*

Giving the home away

In planning for their retirement, some people have tried to make arrangements in advance to give away their property or transfer ownership of their home, with the intention of avoiding the value of the property being taken into account to pay residential care fees. There are considerable risks involved, particularly as there are a number of 'anti-avoidance' measures in the law that enable some gifts of property to be ignored or even set aside by the courts, if they were made specifically with the intention of creating or increasing entitlement to financial assistance from the state.

If the local authority considers that residents have deliberately deprived themselves of their assets in order to obtain help towards the cost of their care, they can assess the residents' contribution as if they still owned the assets, and then take legal proceedings to recover any unpaid contributions. For residents who are receiving Income Support, the value of the assets may again be taken into account, resulting in withdrawal of benefit.

If the person you are acting for is considering giving away any property or valuable assets, he or she should be encouraged to seek independent legal advice on the implications, particularly for future liability to pay residential or nursing home fees. Further information is given in Age Concern Factsheet 40, *Transfer of assets and paying for care in a residential or nursing home.*

What happens to furniture and other belongings?

If there are any belongings that are particularly important to the person you are acting for, you should try to make arrangements for the person to keep these belongings with him or her in the residential or nursing home.

You should also try to find out if any belongings have been promised to a relative or friend (eg in the person's Will). You may have to arrange for these to be looked after until the person dies and probate is granted (see p 114). Anything of value could be taken into account in assessing entitlement to help with fees or Income Support, so may have to be sold to realise their value.

You may have to arrange for the home to be cleared and any contents sold, but you can do this only if you have authority under a power of attorney or are acting with the agreement of the Court of Protection or the Public Trustee.

Death and Dying

The final tasks you may have to carry out in managing other people's affairs will be to deal with the arrangements that have to be made both in preparing for their death and for sorting out their affairs after their death.

People react to thinking about the possibility of death in different ways – some find it morbid, others may see it as a release from suffering, particularly after a long illness. However, if certain practical arrangements have been made to sort out affairs in preparation for death, this can be reassuring for the person who is dying as well as making it easier for those whose task it is to deal with matters afterwards.

Practical arrangements to make before death

Making a Will

The first thing that most people think about in relation to preparing for death is to make a Will – yet few people actually do make one. This may be because they think they do not have enough money or possessions to make it worthwhile, but there are other reasons why it is important to make one.

You cannot make a Will on another person's behalf, but it may be up to you to explain to the person you are acting for why it is so important to make one. Some of the reasons you could give are:

- If people die without making a Will, this is known as dying intestate. Their money, property and possessions will be distributed to members of their family according to certain rules (see p 122), regardless of what they would have wanted.
- Making a Will is the only way to ensure that certain personal possessions (even a pet) are given to a particular relative or friend to have or take care of.
- Making a Will can reduce the amount of tax payable on the inheritance, though it is best to get legal advice on how to do this.

- Making a Will simplifies the administrative work that follows a death. This reduces the time taken to settle an estate as well as the costs involved.
- Making a Will enables people to choose whom they would like to be their executor or personal representative (see p 114), to sort out their affairs after their death.
- Making a Will is the only way that unmarried couples or friends who live together can inherit from each other. If there is no Will, the death of one may cause serious financial problems or even homelessness for the other.
- If a person's circumstances change (eg following marriage or divorce), it is important to make a Will, or change an existing Will, to make sure that money and possessions are distributed according to his or her wishes.
- A Will can include special provision for dependants who cannot care for themselves, such as a child with learning disabilities.

Further information about making a Will can be found in Age Concern Factsheet 7, *Making your will*.

Can everyone make a Will?

Anyone over 18 years can make a Will but, in order for it to be valid, the person must have 'testamentary capacity'. People who have testamentary capacity are of 'sound mind, memory and understanding'. This means they must be fully aware of what they are doing (ie that they will die, what a Will is and that it will come into effect after their death), must understand the extent of the money and property to be disposed of and what will happen to it after their death, and they must be aware of their moral obligations towards the people who might be expected to inherit under the Will, even though they do not have to act on them.

Deciding whether someone has testamentary capacity is not easy. Even a person who is capable of conducting complex business transactions may not have testamentary capacity (eg if he or she suffers from delusions about a close relative who would normally be expected to inherit under the Will), whereas someone with a diagnosed psychiatric illness is not necessarily without testamentary capacity.

If you have any doubt about whether the person you are acting for has the mental capacity to be able to make a Will, it is advisable to seek medical advice. To be on the safe side, a medical expert should be asked to act as a witness to the Will, to show that the person was of sound mind when it was signed.

Statutory Wills

If a person does not have testamentary capacity and is a 'patient' of the Court of Protection (see p 41), it is possible to ask the Court for a 'statutory Will' to be made. This applies to people for whom an enduring power of attorney has been registered (p 27), or a receiver has been appointed (p 43), or a Direction of the Public Trustee has been given (p 53). The procedures for making a statutory Will are complicated, and you should get legal advice. In these cases, the Court can order that a statutory Will is made even though the wishes of the patient are not known. In drafting the Will, the Court will try to carry out what it believes would have been the patient's wishes, if he or she had full mental capacity, memory and foresight.

To make a statutory Will the Court requires specific medical evidence to show that the patient lacks testamentary capacity. The ordinary evidence required for the Court's intervention – that the patient is incapable by reason of mental disorder of managing his or her own affairs (see p 42) – is insufficient. Anyone who would be adversely affected by the proposed statutory Will will be notified of the court hearing and will be able to attend or be represented by a legal adviser, to put his or her views to the Court. The Court will also ensure that the patient is legally represented.

Putting personal papers in order

If the person you are acting for has made a Will, it is important that you know where to find it. However, you are not entitled to know what is in the Will before the person dies, unless he or she has made a point of telling you or has made clear (eg in a power of attorney) that you are allowed access to the Will.

There are other personal papers that you will need to know where to find and be able to deal with if the person whose affairs you are managing dies. It is a good idea to ask their help to collect all these together or make a list with details of where they can be found. This should include:

- details relating to the Will (eg of any wishes concerning the funeral arrangements);
- details of any provision made to cover funeral expenses;
- the Will itself;
- birth, marriage and divorce certificates;
- details of occupational or personal pension schemes;
- insurance policies (eg life assurance, house buildings and contents insurance, car insurance);
- share and investment certificates and details of other investments (eg Premium Bonds, savings certificates, unit trusts);
- property deeds, lease, mortgage details, rent book;
- details of bank, building society and post office accounts, including statements, cheque books, pass books;
- details of credit agreements and credit cards;
- benefit books;
- details of tax office;
- papers relating to any business interests or details of employer(s);
- court orders (eg maintenance orders);
- passport(s);
- safety deposit box and keys;
- details of any trusts of which the person is either a trustee or a beneficiary;
- addresses of professional advisers (eg GP, solicitor, accountant, insurance broker).

It might also be helpful for you to obtain a copy of a leaflet published by Age Concern England, called *Instructions for My Next of Kin*, which is designed to help people prepare for their own death, but covers all the points you may have to take into account in dealing with someone else's affairs. Many solicitors provide a 'Personal Assets Log', which contains similar details.

Putting money or property in joint names

There are certain practical advantages of putting money and property in joint names, particularly for married couples, for the management of their financial affairs during their lifetime (see p 11) and also in the event of their death. These include the following.

Immediate access to money   If money is held in a joint account, the other account holder(s) can continue to draw money after one of them dies. If the account is in the sole name of the person who dies, no one, not even a married partner, will have access to it until probate is granted (see p 114).

Preserving rights to a home   This will depend on whether the property is rented or owned, and how it is owned (whether as joint tenants or tenants in common (see p 120), but the rights of the surviving person will be greater if the property is in joint names (see p 120 for arrangements for dealing with housing after death). If the property is in the sole name of the person who dies, other occupants may not have the right to remain in the home. Legal advice may be needed about this.

It is also important to seek legal advice about putting money or other property in joint names, in order to make the best arrangements according to the particular circumstances you are dealing with. The money or property transferred will not form part of the estate or be available for gifts to other people. Unless the transfer is between husband and wife, the share owned by the person who has died will be taken into account for the payment of Inheritance Tax (see p 118).

Funeral arrangements

Although making funeral arrangements may not be part of your particular responsibilities in managing another person's money, you may be involved if you have to ensure that the costs of the funeral are covered. Many people like to specify how they want their funeral to be arranged, and it is important that their wishes are respected if possible. You should find out whether they have any particular requirements, including:

- whether they wish to be buried or cremated;
- if buried, whether they wish a particular plot to be reserved;
- if cremated, whether the ashes should be buried or scattered;
- what type of service or ceremony (eg religious or secular);
- whether the service should be private or not;
- whether they want flowers or donations to a charity;
- whether there are any particular readings or hymns they would like;

- whether they wish to donate their body or organs for transplant or medical research;
- what they would like to be wearing;
- whether any particular possessions should be buried with them;
- whether a particular funeral director should be used.

Any instructions about funeral arrangements should be left with the Will, and a copy should be left in a place where it can be found and read immediately after the person has died. Information about arranging a funeral is given in Age Concern Factsheet 27, *Arranging a funeral.*

Paying for a funeral

Funerals can be very expensive, and there are several ways in which the cost of a funeral can be met. These are:

- from the estate of the person who has died;
- from a life assurance policy;
- from a pre-payment funeral plan;
- from a Social Fund payment;
- from compensation (eg from the Criminal Injuries Compensation Scheme or under the Fatal Accidents Act);
- from a charity, benevolent fund or trade union covering the occupation of the person who has died;
- by the Ministry of Defence or the Department of Social Security if the person died as a result of active military service or was receiving a War Disablement Pension;
- in certain circumstances, by the local or health authority.

You may wish to consider whether to make arrangements for a pre-payment funeral plan to cover the costs for the person you are acting for. There are three main types of plans.

Bank or **building society accounts** whereby a sum to cover a funeral director's estimated costs is deposited in an interest-bearing account under the funeral director's control. But there is no guarantee that the amount will be sufficient when the person dies.

Whole life assurance policies, which aim to cover the estimated funeral costs at the date of death, allowing for increases with inflation. There is still no guarantee that all the costs will be covered.

Guaranteed pre-arranged funeral plans whereby, for a lump sum payment or fixed regular payments over a number of years, the funeral director agrees to conduct the required funeral without further charge.

There are a number of plans, which vary in price according to the type of funeral and the services required. Further information about pre-payment funeral plans can be obtained from Age Concern England.

Practical arrangements to make after a death

Your responsibilities after the death of the person whose financial affairs you have been managing will depend on what you were originally appointed to do and whether you have been asked to be the 'personal representative' of the person who has died (see p 114). It will usually be the personal representative who is responsible for making all the necessary arrangements after a death.

It is important to note that, if you were appointed under a power of attorney (see p 18), or as a receiver by the Court of Protection (see p 41), your appointment ceases on the death of the donor or patient.

Registering the death

The registration of a death is the formal record that the death has taken place. A death must be registered within five days unless it has been reported to the coroner. The entry in the register will contain details of where and when the death occurred and the cause of death.

Who has to register the death?

Any relative can register the death, but it is usually a close relative and one who was present at the death or during the last days of life. If there are no relatives available, one of the following can register the death:

- a personal representative of the person who has died;
- the hospital, if the death occurred in hospital;
- the proprietor of a residential care or nursing home, if the death occurred there;
- a person living in the same house as the person who has died;
- the person who was present at the death or who found the body.

The doctor or hospital will give the nearest relative or the person present at the death a medical certificate of death, and a 'Notice to Informant' which explains how the death must be registered.

How to register the death

If you have to register the death, it is advisable to make an appointment with the nearest registry of deaths (listed in the telephone directory under 'Registration of Births, Deaths and Marriages'). When you attend the registry to register the death, you must take with you:

- the medical certificate of death, or the form issued by a coroner to show the cause of death (unless these have been sent direct to the registrar);
- the medical card of the person who has died, if available;
- the birth certificate and marriage certificate of the person who has died, if available.

The registrar will also need to know the following details:

- the date and place of death;
- the gender and full names of the person who has died (including a married woman's maiden name);
- the last or usual address of the person who has died;
- the date and place of birth of the person who has died;
- the last full-time occupation of the person who has died;
- the name, occupation and date of birth of the married partner of the person who has died;
- whether the person who has died was getting any Social Security benefits or war pensions.

The registrar will check the details with you before entering them into the register. You and the registrar will then sign the register. The registrar will then provide you with:

- A **certificate for disposal**: this must be given to the funeral director before funeral arrangements can be made.
- The **death certificate**, which is a certified copy of the entry in the register – several copies will be needed when dealing with the estate of the person who has died.
- A **certificate of registration**: this is used for claiming Social Security benefits.

Dealing with property and possessions after a death

The property, money and possessions of the person who has died are known as the 'estate'. The responsibility for sorting out what belongs to the estate, and making the necessary arrangements for the estate to be disposed of, falls to the 'personal representative' of the person who has died. Further information is given in Age Concern Factsheet 14, *Probate: dealing with someone's estate*.

The personal representative

The personal representative is either the person named in the Will as executor of the estate or, if the executor cannot or does not wish to act or the person who has died has not made a Will, someone appointed according to statutory rules, known as an administrator of the estate.

Only certain people can be an administrator. They are:

- Where a Will has been made but executors have not been named, or they cannot or are unwilling to act: the person to whom the whole of the estate has been left, or to whom the residue (remainder of the estate when all gifts have been made) has been left.
- Where there is no Will: the relatives of the person who has died, in the following order of priority: the married partner; children; grand-children; parents; brothers or sisters; nephews or nieces; other relatives

What does the personal representative do?

If you are the personal representative of the person who has died, you are responsible for sorting out his or her affairs, property and posses-sions. However, you will usually have to obtain formal legal authority, known as the 'grant of representation', to act on behalf of that person. There are two types of grant of representation:

- **Probate**, which is given to the executor named in the Will.
- **Letters of administration** (commonly referred to as 'administration'), given to the administrator if there is no Will, or if the Will is not valid, or if executors have not been named or they cannot or are unwilling to act.

A grant of representation is a High Court order, given by the Probate Registry, which confers on you the legal authority to deal with the estate and affairs of the person who has died. In effect, a grant of representation transfers all of the money and property of the person who has died to you, to distribute according to the details set out in the Will, or according to the intestacy rules (see p 122).

As personal representative, you must first ensure that none of the possessions of the person who has died is sold or given away until you have obtained probate or letters of administration. You then take full responsibility for dealing with the estate, which will involve:

- finding out exactly what the assets are in the estate and their value;
- finding out details of any money owed to the estate;
- finding out details of any debts owed by the person who has died;
- preparing a detailed list of the assets and debts in the estate for inheritance tax purposes;
- working out the amount of inheritance tax due and making arrangements to pay this (see p 118);
- preparing and sending off documents required by the Inland Revenue and the Probate Registry;
- checking the probate documents at the Probate Registry;
- collecting assets belonging to the estate from banks, building societies, insurance companies, pension funds etc;
- selling any property, if necessary;
- paying debts, bills, expenses, fees (eg solicitor's fees, probate fees);
- paying legacies and handing over gifts and bequests detailed in the Will or according to the intestacy rules (see p 118);
- distributing or investing the residue (remainder) of the estate.

If the estate is complicated, or if the Will is likely to be contested, it would be advisable to seek legal advice.

When is probate/administration needed?

This depends on the types of assets left by the person who has died and whether these are held in the sole name of that person or jointly with another/others. In most cases, probate/administration will be needed if the estate includes:

- money held in bank, post office or building society accounts;
- a house;
- investments;
- insurance and pension benefits.

Examples of situations in which probate or letters of administration may not be needed are:

- The assets in the estate are made up entirely of cash (bank notes and coins) and personal possessions (eg car, jewellery, furniture).
- All the property in the estate is owned in joint names as joint tenants (see p 120). This means the property automatically becomes wholly owned by the surviving joint tenant.
- All assets are held in joint names (eg bank accounts).
- The total amount of money held in National Savings accounts and pension funds and by insurance companies and building societies is less than £5,000.
- Where a 'nomination agreement' exists. (These agreements could only be made before 1981, and allowed the owner of a property to nominate that it should be passed to a particular person in the event of death.)

Nevertheless, even in cases where probate/administration is not officially needed, there is no obligation for any institution holding money or property on behalf of someone who has died to release it without probate/administration, however small the amount.

How to apply for probate/administration

Whether you are applying for probate or letters of administration, the procedure is the same. The local Probate Registry provides a leaflet, *How to Obtain Probate* (PA 2), which tells you how to complete the relevant application forms, according to the circumstances of the person who has died. The various forms are described below – the current titles and reference numbers are given, but note that these change from time to time.

- The **Probate Application** (Form PA 1) includes details about the person who has died, his or her surviving relatives, the personal representative and details of the Will if there is one.
- **Schedule of land and interest in land** (Form IHT 37) is to be completed if the person who died owned any freehold or leasehold property.

- **Schedule of stocks and shares** (Form IHT 40) is to be completed if the person who died owned any stocks, shares or unit trusts.
- A **return of the whole estate** (Form IHT 44) gives details of the estate and its value, and is used to prepare the account for the Inland Revenue.
- **Spouse's contribution** (Form PA 5) is to be completed if a married partner survives and the home was owned in the sole name of the partner who has died.

Not all these forms may be required, and other forms and leaflets are available to help you make the application. Form PA 3 gives a list of the local Probate Offices and the relevant Probate Registries. Form PA 4 gives details of the fees payable, and when and how to pay them. Form IHT 205, entitled *Short form for a personal applicant – Do you need to complete an Inland Revenue Account before probate?*, helps you to work out whether Inheritance Tax is likely to be payable, and whether it will be necessary to complete Form IHT 44, *A return of the whole estate*.

The completed forms should be returned, either personally or by Recorded delivery, to the local Probate Registry, together with the original Will (if there is one), a copy of the death certificate, and all the relevant supporting documents, such as letters confirming the value of the assets. You should keep copies of all the forms.

Once the Probate Registry has prepared all the legal documents, you will be asked to attend at the Registry for an interview with a commissioner. You will then be asked to check through all the documents, as you are responsible for ensuring that they are accurate. Once satisfied that the details are correct, you will be asked to sign the oath (a document prepared by the Probate Registry from the answers given on the various application forms), and the original Will if there is one. You will then be asked to swear or affirm that you have signed the oath, that the details are correct and that the Will is the correct one. The commissioner will then also sign the forms and the Will.

You will then have to pay the fee due, which will depend on the net value of the estate. You will also have to order official copies of the probate/administration document, which have the court's seal on them to prove their authenticity. You may need several copies of the document as proof of your authority to enable you to carry out the settlement of the estate, although one may be used by several institutions, being stamped and returned by each in turn.

Inheritance Tax

Inheritance Tax is a tax on the value of the estate, which is payable if the value is more than a certain amount. This amount is usually raised each year in the Budget, and the amount that applies is the one in force at the date of death, not when the estate is finally settled.

Once the tax-free amount has been exceeded, gifts made by the person in the seven years before his or her death will be added together, to give the figure on which Inheritance Tax will be levied. However, there are certain exemptions; for example, gifts between husband and wife, whatever their value, and gifts to other people below a certain level or, in particular circumstances, gifts to charities and political parties. Further information is given in Inland Revenue leaflet IR 45, *What to do about tax when someone dies.*

The tax has to be paid before probate/administration is granted, but it is not always possible to use money from the estate to pay the tax until you have the probate/administration document. Therefore, you may need to make arrangements to raise money to pay for the Inheritance Tax as well as the probate fees. If the person who died had National Savings investments or government stocks, you might be able to obtain the funds needed by applying to the Department of National Savings. Alternatively, banks or building societies may agree to release money from an account held by the person who died, or to grant a loan, but they are not obliged to do so.

Once probate/administration has been granted, a final assessment of the Inheritance Tax is made, and any further payment due can be taken from the estate.

Executorship accounts

It would be advisable for you to open a separate bank or building society account, known as an 'executorship account', into which the money paid into the estate can be credited. (This could include any money from the deceased person's bank and building society accounts, life assurance, pension arrears or other payments from pension funds, tax refunds, dividends due on shares, any other savings or investments, money from the sale of property or other assets etc.) If this is done, the bank or building society will often agree to lend the money required to pay the tax and probate fees, if you can show that the estate will be of sufficient value to cover the loan.

Settling the estate

Once all the application procedures have been completed and the Inheritance Tax and probate fees have been paid, the 'grant of representation' will be issued in the form of the probate/administration document. The document will be sent to you, with a statement of the gross and net estate (before and after debts have been deducted), and a copy of the Will stamped to prove it is an official copy. The original Will will be kept at Somerset House, London.

You can now begin to settle the estate and arrange for the distribution of property and possessions. You will need to do the following:

- obtain all the assets belonging to the estate;
- pay the outstanding debts of the estate;
- finalise the payment of taxes;
- dispose of any unwanted property, in particular by selling anything of value;
- distribute the estate to friends, relatives, etc, according to the terms of the Will or the rules of intestacy (see p 122);
- return any borrowed property (eg library books, NHS equipment).

Paying the debts

Any debts must usually be settled first. In some cases, it may be necessary to advertise for creditors in the local newspaper to ensure that all debts are paid before the assets are distributed. If it appears that there may not be sufficient money in the estate to cover all the debts, you should seek advice from a solicitor. You may need to consider selling property such as housing or investments to raise money to pay the debts. Some creditors will have priority, as follows:

- mortgagees and others who have lent money secured on land;
- Inland Revenue for Inheritance, Income and Capital Gains Taxes;
- local authority for Council Tax.

Creditors who do not have priority are entitled to a proportion of the amount owed to them if there is insufficient money left in the estate to settle the whole debt.

As the personal representative, you are also entitled to deduct your expenses from the estate, as follows:

- costs of copies of the grant of probate administration;
- stamp duty and charges incurred in transferring shares and property;
- out-of-pocket expenses (eg travel, postage).

You are not entitled to charge for the time taken or the work involved in dealing with the estate.

Dealing with investments

If the person who has died held investments, you will have to arrange for these to be sold or transferred to the beneficiaries entitled to inherit them. If shares were owned and have to be sold to pay off debts, you will need to use a stockbroker, as stocks and shares cannot be sold direct. The broker's fees will be deducted from the money raised by the sale. You should keep a record of details of the fees and the prices at which the shares were sold.

If the shares are to be transferred, you will need to complete the relevant form, available from the Probate Registry (Form IHT 40) when applying for probate/administration.

Dealing with housing

Owned property

You may have to arrange the sale or transfer of any property owned by the person who has died. If he or she was the sole owner, the property will pass according to the terms of the Will or the intestacy rules.

If the person who has died owned the property jointly with others, what happens to the property depends on whether they owned it as joint tenants or as tenants-in-common:

- In the case of a **joint tenancy**, ownership passes automatically to the surviving joint tenant(s) on the death of a co-owner, irrespective of the provisions of the Will. No formalities are required, other than

Inheritance tax

In his Budget speech, the Chancellor proposed to raise the
threshold for inheritance tax from £90,000 to £110,000 and to
replace the present four rates of tax with a single rate of 40%
for a net estate above £110,000 (irrespective of size of
estate).

Existing scale		Proposed scale
Range (£000s) to which tax applies	Rate of tax per cent	Range (£000s) to which tax applies
0 - 90	NIL	0 - 110
over 90 - 140	30	-
over 140 - 220	40	above 110
over 220 - 330	50	-
above 330	60	-

The Chancellor also proposed to abolish the £100,000 exemption
limit on gifts to political parties, made on or within one year
of death. A political party is eligible for the exemption if, at
the last general election before the gift, two members were
elected to the House of Commons or one member was so elected and
at least 150,000 votes were given to candidates who were members
of the party.

The information and calculations in this book should be read in
the light of these changes which are to apply to the estate of
anyone who died on or after 15 March 1988.

Income tax and Capital gains tax (CGT)

The CGT exemption figure will be £5,000 and the tax on gains
above that amount will be at the same rate as the basic rate of
income tax (25% from April 1988).

sending a copy of the death certificate, to be kept with the title deeds or charge certificate (see below).

- In the case of a **tenancy-in-common**, the share of the property owned by the person who has died will pass according to the terms of the Will or under intestacy rules. This may mean that the property will have to be sold to realise the share owned by the person who has died.

The legal procedure for transferring property varies according to whether or not the property is built on land which, for historical reasons, is registered with the Land Registry.

If the land is registered, ownership is established in a land certificate, held by the Land Registry. If there is a mortgage, the lender will hold a charge certificate, which will be returned to the owner or owner's personal representative when the mortgage has been paid off. To effect a sale or transfer, the charge certificate and an official acknowledgement from the lender that the mortgage has been paid off should be sent to the Land Registry, who will then issue the land certificate to the personal representative so that the property can be sold, or transferred into the name of the beneficiary.

If the land is not registered, ownership of the property is established in the title deeds, which will be kept by the lender if there is a mortgage, or by the owner or owner's solicitor if there is not. Transferring unregistered property can be complicated and it is advisable to use a solicitor. A document called an 'assent' needs to be drawn up, whereby the personal representative assents to the transfer of the property into the beneficiary's name.

Rented property

If other relatives were living in rented accommodation with the person who has died, they may have the right to succeed to (take over) the tenancy, and remain in the property. It is best to seek advice from an advice agency or a solicitor, as rights of succession will depend on the type of tenancy as well as individual circumstances.

Distributing the estate

After paying all the debts of the estate and finalising the payment of Inheritance Tax, you can distribute the remaining property and possessions from the estate, either according to the terms of the Will or under the intestacy rules if there is no Will.

You should ensure that you obtain a signed receipt from each beneficiary who receives something from the estate. Once distribution has been completed, you should do a final check of all the money paid in, all the payments made out and all the expenses charged to the estate. You should then prepare the estate accounts, which must be approved and signed by you and the main beneficiaries. You will then know how much is left in the residue (remainder) of the estate, which can also be distributed to the main beneficiary.

Intestacy

There are special rules to follow when distributing the estate of a person who has died without leaving a Will. These rules favour the married partner and close blood-relations of the person who has died. People related by marriage, friends or cohabiting partners have no rights to inherit under the rules.

Under the intestacy rules, the property and possessions of the estate must be distributed to the next surviving relatives of the person who has died, in the following order of priority:

- married partner;
- children (or grandchildren if the children have died);
- parents;
- brothers and sisters (or their children if they have died);
- half brothers and sisters (or their children if they have died);
- grandparents;
- uncles and aunts (or their children if they have died);
- half uncles and aunts (or their children if they have died);
- the Crown.

In general, most of the estate will go to the surviving married partner and any children of the person who has died. In particular, the married partner will receive everything up to the first £125,000; if the estate is worth more than this, provision is made for any children. If there are no children, the married partner receives everything up to £200,000, after which provision is made for the next surviving relatives. These figures change from time to time.

There are further rules that determine how the property should be distributed, which depend on the value of the net estate (after the deduction of taxes, debts, legal costs, probate fees and other expenses) and which relatives survive the person who has died.

This is merely a rough outline of the intestacy rules. If the person you are acting for has died without making a Will, you should seek advice from a solicitor as to how the rules apply in his or her individual case.

Points
to Note

This section provides checklists of points to note when you are managing other people's money and financial affairs. Most of them are common sense, but it is worthwhile making an effort to follow them — not only for the sake of the person whose affairs you are managing but also as a safeguard for yourself against allegations of abuse.

Checklists

Procedures

Try to put yourself in the position of the person whose affairs you are looking after. As far as possible, do what you think that person would have done, if he or she had been able to.

So far as possible, follow the wishes of the person you are acting for. These wishes may have been expressed in various ways:

- in a power of attorney;
- in a trust deed;
- in a Will;
- informally, while the person was still capable of managing alone, or during a lucid period.

Always consult with the person you are acting for and take time to explain what you are doing, even if you don't think he or she can understand. Most people who are considered mentally incapable of managing their own affairs will be able to understand some things, at some times better than others. It will reassure them to know what is going on even if they forget later.

When you are acting in a formal capacity (eg as an attorney, a receiver or as the personal representative of someone who has died), take care to follow the correct procedures. You may be acting illegally if you fail to do so.

Use money wisely, but don't be mean! There is no point storing up money that could be used for the benefit and comfort of the person you are acting for.

Safeguards

Always keep careful records of what you are doing, for your own reference. You should record details of any income you have received, any money you have spent and what you have spent it on, bills you have paid and any other financial transactions you have carried out. This includes keeping regular, up-to-date accounts, so that you always have a good idea what the person's current financial position is.

Keep the person's money in a separate bank or building society account held in his or her name, so that it doesn't get mixed up with your own – unless you are acting for your husband or wife and have decided that the best arrangement for you is to keep money in joint names.

When dealing with savings, investments or property, make sure you have the proper authority. This will normally be either from the person who owns it, under a power of attorney, or from the Court of Protection or the Public Trustee.

If you are in any doubt about what you are doing, or if the financial affairs of the person you are acting for are complicated in any way, always seek advice.

Complaints

If you think that someone else is acting wrongly in managing the money or affairs of another person, who is not capable of acting for him- or herself, report it to the relevant authorities.

- If it concerns the collection or use of Social Security benefits, complain to the local Benefits Agency office.
- If it concerns a power of attorney, complain to the Public Trust Office.
- If it concerns someone who has been appointed as a receiver, complain to the Public Trust Office.
- If it concerns a solicitor, complain to the Office for the Supervision of Solicitors.
- If it concerns the proprietor of a residential or nursing home, complain to the registration authority.
- If it concerns someone you think is using or interfering with another person's money or property without proper authority, complain to the Public Trust Office.

If you need help in taking up a complaint, or in relation to any other problem concerned with managing another person's money:

- ask for help from your local Citizens Advice Bureau or other advice agency;
- seek advice from a solicitor – Legal Aid may be available;
- ask for help from the local social services department;
- contact the Customer Services Unit of the Public Trust Office. The Public Trust Office will ensure that the Court of Protection is made aware of any problems requiring the Court's intervention.

Further Information

This part of the book provides details of local sources of help and gives the addresses of organisations that can be contacted for assistance and advice. A comprehensive recommended reading list has also been included with details of other publications to which readers can turn if they need further information about a particular subject.

Information is also provided about Age Concern and its collection of publications and factsheets.

An index has been included to help you find your way around this book.

Sources of Help

Helpful organisations

Age Concern (Old People's Welfare)

Most areas have an Age Concern group that provides services and advice. Look in the phone book under 'Age Concern' but if you can't find an address, ask your local Citizens Advice Bureau or library, or write for the address of your local group to the relevant national Age Concern office (addresses on page 153).

Citizens Advice Bureaux (CABx)

The local bureaux provide advice and information on all kinds of problems. Some bureaux can arrange home visits. Some can give legal advice, and they will also give you the names of local solicitors, particularly those who do Legal Aid work. Look in the phone book under 'Citizens Advice Bureau'.

Solicitors

The Law Society publishes the Solicitors Regional Directory for England and Wales, which sets out the names and addresses of local solicitors, the areas of law and the type of work they do, and whether they operate the Legal Aid scheme. CABx, local libraries and advice agencies should have the directory.

Law centres

There may be a law centre giving free legal advice in your area. Check in the phone book or at the CAB. Law centres are also listed in the Solicitors Regional Directories.

Independent and money advice centres

There may be an independent advice centre in your area that gives free advice on welfare rights and other problems. Money advice centres generally deal with debt problems and may only accept referrals from other agencies. Advice centres are also listed in the Solicitors Regional Directory.

Community Relations Councils (CRCs)

Local CRCs will give help and advice to people from black and ethnic minorities. Look in the phone book or contact the Commission for Racial Equality (see p 132) for the address of your local CRC.

Local council

You should contact your local council (local authority) about the provision of social services (including residential care or help at home), Housing Benefit and Council Tax Benefit. Look up the address in the phone book under the name of your area, borough, district or region.

Useful addresses

Some of the national organisations listed below may be able to put you in touch with a source of advice.

Age Concern England
1268 London Road
London SW16 4ER
Tel: 0181-679 8000

Alzheimer's Disease Society
Gordon House
10 Greencoat Place
London SW1P 1PH
Tel: 0171-306 0606

Benefits Agency
Quarry House
Quarry Hill
Leeds LS2 7UA

(*For local Benefits Agency offices, look in the phone book under 'Benefits Agency'*)

Building Societies Association
3 Savile Row
London W1X 1AP
Tel: 0171-437 0655

Capital Taxes Office
Ferrers House
PO Box 38
Castle Meadow Road
Nottingham NG2 1BB
Tel: 0115-974 2400

Carers National Association
20 Glasshouse Yard
London EC1A 1JS
Tel: 0171-490 8898

Child Poverty Action Group
1–5 Bath Street
London EC1V 9PY
Tel: 0171-253 3406

Commission for Racial Equality
Elliot House
10–12 Allington Street
London SW1E 5EH
Tel: 0171-828 7022

Counsel and Care for the Elderly
Twyman House
16 Bonny Street
London NW1 9CR
Tel: 0171-485 1566

Court of Protection
Stewart House
24 Kingsway
London WC2B 6HD
Tel: 0171-664 7000

CRUSE – Bereavement Care
Cruse House
126 Sheen Road
Richmond
Surrey TW9 1UR
Tel: 0181-940 4818

Department of National Savings
375 Kensington High Street
London W14 8SD
Tel: 0171-605 9461

Department of Social Security
Pensions and Overseas Benefits Directorate
Tyneview Park
Whitley Road
Benton
Newcastle-upon-Tyne NE98 1BA
Tel: 0191-203 0203

Attendance Allowance Unit
Warbreck House
Blackpool FY5 3AW
Tel: 01345 123 456

Disability Alliance
88–94 Wentworth Street
London E1 7SA
Tel: 0171-247 8776

Disability Law Service
49 Bedford Row
London WC1R 4LR
Tel: 0171-831 8031

Disabled Living Foundation
380 Harrow Road
London W9 4LR
Tel: 0171-289 6111

Elderly Accommodation Council
46A Chiswick High Road
London W4 1SZ
Tel: 0181-995 8320 or 0181-742 1182

Federation of Independent Advice Centres
London Unit
13 Stockwell Road
London SW9 9AU
Tel: 0171-274 1839

Financial Services Authority (FSA)
(*formerly* Securities and Investment Board)
Gavrelle House
2–14 Bunhill Row
London EC1Y 8RA
Tel: 0171-929 3652

IMRO (Investment Managers Regulatory Organisation)
Lloyds Chambers
1 Portsoken Street
London E1 8BT
Tel: 0171-390 5000

Independent Living Fund
PO Box 183
Nottingham NG8 3RD
Tel: 0115-942 8191

Inland Revenue
Somerset House
The Strand
London WC2R 1LB
Tel: 0171-438 6622

(*Tax affairs are dealt with by different tax offices, but enquiries can be made to the nearest tax office. Look in the phone book under 'Inland Revenue'*)

Insurance Ombudsman
135 Park Street
London SE1 9EA
Tel: 0171-928 4488

Law Society
113 Chancery Lane
London WC2A 1PL
Tel: 0171-242 1222

MENCAP (Royal Society for Mentally Handicapped Children and Adults)
Mencap National Centre
123 Golden Lane
London EC1Y 0RT
Tel: 0171-454 0451

MIND (National Association for Mental Health)
15–19 Broadway
London E15 4BQ
Tel: 0181-519 2122

National Association of Widows
54–57 Allison Street
Birmingham B5 5TH
Tel: 0121-643 8348

National Consumer Council
20 Grosvenor Gardens
London SW1W 0DH
Tel: 0171-730 3469

National Federation of Retirement Pensions Associations
(Pensioners' Voice)
14 St Peters Street
Blackburn BB2 2HD
Tel: 01254 52606

Office of the Banking Ombudsman
70 Gray's Inn Road
London WC1X 8NB
Tel: 0171-404 9944

Office of the Building Societies Ombudsman
Millbank Tower
Millbank
London SW1P 4XG
Tel: 0171-931 0044

Office for the Supervision of Solicitors (OSS)
Victoria Court
8 Dormer Place
Leamington Spa
Warwickshire CV32 5AE
Tel: 01926 822007

Pensions Advisory Service (OPAS)
11 Belgrave Road
London SW1V 1RB
Tel: 0171-233 8080

Pension Schemes Registry
PO Box 1NN
Newcastle-upon-Tyne NE99 1NN
Tel: 0191-225 6393/6394

Personal Investment Authority (PIA)
7th Floor
1 Canada Square
Canary Wharf
London E14 5AZ
Tel: 0171-538 8860

PIA Ombudsman
Hertsmere House
Hertsmere Road
London E14 4AB
Tel: 0171-216 0016

Public Trust Office
Stewart House
24 Kingsway
London WC2B 6HD
Tel: 0171-664 7300

Royal National Institute for the Blind
224 Great Portland Street
London W1N 6AA
Tel: 0171-388 1266

Royal National Institute for Deaf People
105 Gower Street
London WC1E 6AH
Tel: 0171-387 8033

Securities and Futures Authority (SFA)
Cotton Centre
Cottons Lane
London SE1 2QB
Tel: 0171-378 9000

Securities and Investment Board (SIB)
see Financial Services Authority

Stock Exchange
Old Broad Street
London EC1N 1HP
Tel: 0171-588 2355

Useful Publications

Further reading

Further information about the Age Concern England publications listed in this section can be found on pages 154–156.

The powers available

Books

Elderly People and the Law by G Ashton, published by Butterworths, London, 1995

Enduring Powers of Attorney, 4th edition, by S Cretney and D Lush, published by Jordans, Bristol, 1996

Court of Protection Handbook, 10th edition, by A Donnelly, published by FT Law & Tax, London, 1995

Court of Protection Practice by L Hine, published by CLT Professional Publishing, Birmingham, 1997

Leaflets

Age Concern England:

Factsheet 22: *Legal arrangements for managing financial affairs*

Public Trust Office:

Enduring Powers of Attorney – An explanatory booklet

Making an Application

Handbook for Receivers

Duties of a Receiver

Fees

Information for nursing homes, hospitals and other carers

Factsheet 1, *Accounts*

Factsheet 2, *Annual Enquiry*

Factsheet 3, *Investments*

Factsheet 4, *Death of an incapacitated person*

Factsheet 5, *Applying for a Direction of the Public Trustee*

All available from the address on p 136.

Social Security benefits and pensions

Books

Your Rights – A guide to money benefits for older people, published annually by Age Concern England.

Disability Rights Handbook, published annually by the Disability Alliance. Available from the address on p 133.

National Welfare Benefits Handbook, published annually by the Child Poverty Action Group (CPAG). Available from the address on p 132.

Rights Guide to Non-Means-Tested Security Benefits, published annually by Child Poverty Action Group (CPAG). Available from the address on p 132.

Leaflets

Age Concern England:

Factsheet 16: *Income related benefits: income and capital*

Factsheet 17: *Housing Benefit and Council Tax Benefit*

Factsheet 18: *A brief guide to money benefits*

Factsheet 21: *The Council Tax and older people*

Factsheet 25: *Income Support and the Social Fund*

Factsheet 34: *Attendance Allowance and Disability Living Allowance*

Department of Social Security and Benefits Agency:

Leaflets are available from the post office and the local Benefits Agency office.

Taxation, savings and investments

Books

Your Taxes and Savings – A guide for older people, published annually by Age Concern England

Leaflets

Age Concern England:

Factsheet 15: *Income tax and older people*

Inland Revenue:

Various leaflets are available from the local tax office or Citizens Advice Bureau, including:

Income Tax and Pensioners (IR 121)

A guide for widows and widowers (IR 91)

Capital Gains Tax: An introduction (CGT 14)

Inheritance Tax: An introduction (IHT 3)

Self Assessment: A general guide (SA/BK1)

Other financial matters

Books

Using Your Home as Capital by C Hinton, published annually by Age Concern England.

Leaflets

Age Concern England:

Factsheet 12: *Raising income and capital from your home*

Living arrangements

Books

A Buyer's Guide to Retirement Housing, published by Age Concern England and the National Housing and Town Planning Council.

Rights Guide for Home Owners, published annually by the Child Poverty Action Group (CPAG)/London Housing Aid Centre (SHAC). Available from the address on p 132.

Leaflets

Age Concern England:

Factsheet 2: *Retirement housing for sale*

Factsheet 8: *Rented accommodation for older people*

Factsheet 13: *Older home owners: financial help with repairs and adaptations*

Department of the Environment:

Assured and assured shorthold tenancies: a guide for tenants

Regulated tenancies

Home repair assistance

Available from DoE Publications, Despatch Centre, Blackhorse Road, London SE99 6TT

Community and residential care

Books

Community Care and the Law by L Clements, published by Legal Action Group, 1997 (address: 242 Pentonville Road, London N1 9UN)

Signposts through the Maze: A guide to carers and the law by L Clements and G Ruan, published by Carers National Association. Available from the address on p 132

A Better Home Life – A code of good practice for residential and nursing home care, published by Centre for Policy on Ageing, 1996 (address: 25–31 Ironmonger Row, London EC1V 3QP)

Leaflets

Age Concern England:

Factsheet 6: *Finding help at home*

Factsheet 10: *Local authority charging procedures for residential and nursing home care*

Factsheet 11: *Financial support for people in residential and nursing home care prior to 1 April 1993*

Factsheet 29: *Finding residential and nursing home accommodation*

Death and dying

Books

What to Do When Someone Dies by P Harris

Wills and Probate

How to sort out someone's will: a straightforward guide to coping with probate

These are *Which?* Consumer Guides, available from Which? Ltd, Freepost, Hertford X, SG14 1LH

Leaflets

Age Concern England:

Factsheet 7: *Making your will*

Factsheet 14: *Probate: dealing with someone's estate*

Factsheet 27: *Arranging a funeral*

Department of Social Security/Benefits Agency

Help When Someone Dies: What to do after a death. Available from the local Benefits Agency office

Law Society:

Making a Will Won't Kill You. Available from the address on p 135.

Probate Registry:

How to Obtain Probate. Available from the Probate Personal Application Department, South Wing, Somerset House, Strand, London WC2R lLP, or from the local Probate Registry.

Appendix I
Ordinary Power of Attorney: standard form

THIS GENERAL POWER OF ATTORNEY is made this   day of   19

by [full name of donor   ] of [address of donor   ]

I appoint [full name of attorney   ] of [address of attorney   ]

(or [name   ] of [address   ]

and [name   ] of [address   ]

jointly/jointly and severally)

to be my attorney[s] in accordance with section 10 of the Powers of Attorney Act 1971.

IN WITNESS whereof I have hereto signed this instrument as my deed in the presence of the person[s] mentioned below.

SIGNED AS A DEED AND DELIVERED

by the said [name of donor   ] of [signature of donor   ]

in the presence of [full name of witness   ] of [address   ]

[occupation or description   ]

[Signature of witness   ]

Appendix 2
Enduring Power of Attorney form

SCHEDULE   Regulations 2.and 3

ENDURING POWER OF ATTORNEY

Part A: About using this form

1. **You may choose one attorney or more than one.** If you choose one attorney then you must delete everything between the square brackets on the first page of the form. If you choose more than one, you must decide whether they are able to act:
   - Jointly (that is, they must all act together and cannot act separately) or
   - Jointly and severally (that is, they can all act together but they can also act separately if they wish).

   On the first page of the form, show what you have decided by crossing out one of the alternatives.

2. **If you give your attorney(s) general power** in relation to all your property and affairs, it means that they will be able to deal with your money or property and may be able to sell your house.

3. **If you don't want your attorney(s) to have such wide powers,** you can include any restrictions you like. For example, you can include a restriction that your attorney(s) must not act on your behalf until they have reason to believe that you are becoming mentally incapable; or a restriction as to what your attorney(s) may do. Any restrictions you choose must be written or typed where indicated on the second page of the form.

4. **If you are a trustee** (and please remember that co-ownership of a home involves trusteeship), you should seek legal advice if you want your attorney(s) to act as a trustee on your behalf.

5. **Unless you put in a restriction preventing it** your attorney(s) will be able to use any of your money or property to make any provision which you yourself might be expected to make for their own needs or the needs of other people. Your attorney(s) will also be able to use your money to make gifts, but only for reasonable amounts in relation to the value of your money and property.

6. **Your attorney(s) can recover the out-of-pocket expenses** of acting as your attorney(s). If your attorney(s) are professional people, for example solicitors or accountants, they may be able to charge for their professional services as well. You may wish to provide expressly for remuneration of your attorney(s) (although if they are trustees they may not be allowed to accept it).

7. **If your attorney(s) have reason to believe** that you have become or are becoming mentally incapable of managing your affairs, your attorney(s) will have to apply to the Court of Protection for registration of this power.

8. **Before applying to the Court of Protection for registration** of this power, your attorney(s) must give written notice that that is what they are going to do, to you and your nearest relatives as defined in the Enduring Powers of Attorney Act 1985. You or your relatives will be able to object if you or they disagree with registration.

9. **This is a simplified explanation** of what the Enduring Powers of Attorney Act 1985 and the Rules and Regulations say. If you need more guidance, you or your advisers will need to look at the Act itself and the Rules and Regulations. The Rules are the Court of Protection (Enduring Powers of Attorney) Rules 1986 (Statutory Instrument 1986 No. 127). The Regulations are the Enduring Powers of Attorney (Prescribed Form) Regulations 1990 (Statutory Instrument 1990 No. 1376).

10. **Note to Attorney(s)**
    After the power has been registered you should notify the Court of Protection if the donor dies or recovers.

11. **Note to Donor**
    Some of these explanatory notes may not apply to the form you are using if it has already been adapted to suit your particular requirements.

YOU CAN CANCEL THIS POWER AT ANY TIME BEFORE IT HAS TO BE REGISTERED

Part B: To be completed by the 'donor' (the person appointing the attorney(s))

Don't sign this form unless you understand what it means

Please read the notes in the margin which follow and which are part of the form itself.

Donor's name and address.

I _____

of _____

Donor's date of birth.

born on _____

appoint _____

See note 1 on the front of this form. If you are appointing only one attorney you should cross out everything between the square brackets. If appointing more than two attorneys please give the additional name(s) on an attached sheet.

of _____

• [and _____

  of _____

Cross out the one which does not apply (see note 1 on the front of this form).

- jointly
- jointly and severally]

to be my attorney(s) for the purpose of the Enduring Powers of Attorney Act 1985

Cross out the one which does not apply (see note 2 on the front of this form). Add any additional powers.

- with general authority to act on my behalf
- with authority to do the following on my behalf:

If you don't want the attorney(s) to have general power, you must give details here of what authority you are giving the attorney(s).

in relation to

Cross out the one which does not apply.

- all my property and affairs:
- the following property and affairs:

Part B: continued

Please read the notes in the margin which follow and which are part of the form itself.
If there are restrictions or conditions, insert them here; if not, cross out these words if you wish (see note 3 on the front of this form).

• subject to the following restrictions and conditions:

If this form is being signed at your direction:–
• the person signing must not be an attorney or any witness (to Parts B or C).
• you must add a statement that this form has been signed at your direction.
• a second witness is necessary (please see below).

Your signature (or mark).

I intend that this power shall continue even if I become mentally incapable

I have read or have had read to me the notes in Part A which are part of, and explain, this form.

Signed by me as a deed _____
and delivered

Date.
Someone must witness your signature.

Signature of witness.

Your attorney(s) cannot be your witness. It is not advisable for your husband or wife to be your witness.

on_____

in the presence of _____

Full name of witness_____

Address of witness _____

_____

_____

A second witness is only necessary if this form is not being signed by you personally but at your direction (for example, if a physical disability prevents you from signing).
Signature of second witness.

in the presence of _____

Full name of witness_____

Address of witness _____

_____

_____

Further Information

Part C: To be completed by the attorney(s)

Note: 1. This form may be adapted to provide for execution by a corporation
2. If there is more than one attorney additional sheets in the form as shown below must be added to this Part C

Please read the notes in the margin which follow and which are part of the form itself.

Don't sign this form before the donor has signed Part B or if, in your opinion, the donor was already mentally incapable at the time of signing Part B.

If this form is being signed at your direction:–
• the person signing must not be an attorney or any witness (to Parts B or C).
• you must add a statement that this form has been signed at your direction.
• a second witness is necessary (please see below).

Signature (or mark) of attorney.

Date.

Signature of witness.

The attorney must sign the form and his signature must be witnessed. The donor may not be the witness and one attorney may not witness the signature of the other.

A second witness is only necessary if this form is not being signed by you personally but at your direction (for example, if a physical disability prevents you from signing).
Signature of second witness.

I understand that I have a duty to apply to the Court for the registration of this form under the Enduring Powers of Attorney Act 1985 when the donor is becoming or has become mentally incapable.

I also understand my limited power to use the donor's property to benefit persons other than the donor.

I am not a minor

Signed by me as a deed _____
and delivered

on_____

in the presence of _____

Full name of witness_____

Address of witness _____

_____

_____

in the presence of _____

Full name of witness_____

Address of witness _____

_____

_____

Appendix 3
Enduring Power of Attorney: notice of intention to apply for registration

SCHEDULE 1   Rule 3

FORM EP1

Court of Protection/Public Trust Office

Enduring Powers of Attorney Act 1985

Notice of intention to apply for registration

To ....

of ....

TAKE NOTICE THAT

This form may be adapted for use by three or more attorneys.

I...

of...

and I ....

of...

Give the name and address of the donor.

the attorney(s) of...

....

of..

....

It will be necessary for you to produce evidence in support of your objection. If evidence is available please send it with your objection, the attorney(s) will be given an opportunity to respond to your objection.

intend to apply to the Public Trustee for registration of the enduring power of attorney appointing me (us) attorney(s) and made by the donor on the .... 19..............

1. If you wish to object to the proposed registration you have 4 weeks from the day on which this notice is given to you to do so in writing. Any objections should be sent to the Public Trustee and should contain the following details:

- your name and address;

- any relationship to the donor;

- if you are not the donor, the name and address of the donor;

- the name and address of the attorney;

The grounds upon which you can object are limited and are shown at 2 overleaf.

- the grounds for objecting to the registration of the enduring power.

EP1

149

Note. The instrument means the enduring power of attorney made by the donor which it is sought to register.	2. The grounds on which you may object are: • that the power purported to have been created by the instrument is not valid as an enduring power of attorney; • that the power created by the instrument no longer subsists; • that the application is premature because the donor is not yet becoming mentally incapable; • that fraud or undue pressure was used to induce the donor to make the power; • that the attorney is unsuitable to be the donor's attorney (having regard to all the circumstances and in particular the attorney's relationship to or connection with the donor).
The attorney(s) does not have to be a relative. Relatives are not entitled to know of the existence of the enduring power of attorney prior to being given this notice.	

Note. This is addressed only to the donor.	3. You are informed that while the enduring power of attorney remains registered, you will not be able to revoke it until the Court of Protection confirms the revocation.

Note. This notice should be signed by every one of the attorneys who are applying to register the enduring power of attorney.	Signed .... Dated .... Signed .... Dated ....

Appendix 4
Enduring Power of Attorney: application for registration

FORM EP2

Court of Protection/Public Trust Office　　No. ....

Enduring Powers of Attorney Act 1985

Application for registration

Note. Give the full name and present adddress of the donor. If the donor's address on the enduring power of attorney is different give that one too.	**The donor** Name .... Address .... Address on the Enduring Power of Attorney (if different)............ ....
Note. Give the full name(s) and details of the attorney(s)	**The attorney(s)** Name .... Address .... age ....occupation .... relationship to donor (if any) ....
This form may be adapted for use by three or more attorneys	Name .... Address .... age ....occupation .... relationship to donor (if any) ....
The date is the date upon which the donor signed the enduring power of attorney	I (we) the attorney(s) apply to register the enduring power of attorney made by the donor under the above Act on the... 19 .... the original of which accompanies this application
	I (we) have reason to believe that the donor is or is becoming mentally incapable
Notice must be personally given. It should be made clear if someone other than the attorney(s) gives the notice	I (we) have given notice in the prescribed form to the following: _____ • the donor personally at .... on the... 19 ....

EP2

• The following relatives of the donor at the addresses below on the dates given:

<table>
<tr><td>If there are no relatives entitled to notice please say so</td><td>Names</td><td>Relationship</td><td>addresses</td><td>date</td></tr>
<tr><td></td><td></td><td></td><td></td><td></td></tr>
</table>

Note. Cross out this section if it does not apply.

• The Co-Attorney(s) ....

at ....

on ....

A remittance for the registration fee accompanies this application

Note. The application should be signed by all the attorneys who are making the application.

I (we) certify that the above information is correct and that to the best of my (our) knowledge and belief I (we) have complied with the provisions of the Enduring Powers of Attorney Act 1985 and of all the Rules and Regulations under it.

Signed..Dated ....

This must not pre-date the date(s) when the notices were given

Signed..Dated ....

....

Address to which correspondence relating to the application is to be sent if different to that of the first-named attorney making this application. ....

....

About Age Concern

Managing Other People's Money is one of a wide range of publications produced by Age Concern England, the National Council on Ageing. Age Concern cares about all older people and believes later life should be fulfilling and enjoyable. For too many this is impossible. As the leading charitable movement in the UK concerned with ageing and older people, Age Concern finds effective ways to change that situation.

Where possible, we enable older people to solve problems themselves, providing as much or as little support as they need. Our network of 1,400 local groups, supported by 250,000 volunteers, provides community-based services such as lunch clubs, day centres and home visiting.

Nationally, we take a lead role in campaigning, parliamentary work, policy analysis, research, specialist information and advice provision, and publishing. Innovative programmes promote healthier lifestyles and provide older people with opportunities to give the experience of a lifetime back to their communities.

Age Concern is dependent on donations, covenants and legacies.

Age Concern England
1268 London Road
London SW16 4ER
Tel: 0181-679 8000

Age Concern Scotland
113 Rose Street
Edinburgh EH2 3DT
Tel: 0131-220 3345

Age Concern Cymru
4th Floor
1 Cathedral Road
Cardiff CF1 9SD
Tel: 01222 371566

Age Concern Northern Ireland
3 Lower Crescent
Belfast BT7 1NR
Tel: 01232 245729

Publications from Age Concern Books

MONEY MATTERS

Your Rights: A guide to money benefits for older people

Sally West

A highly successful, popular book – now in its 25th edition – *Your Rights* ensures that older people – and their advisers – can easily understand the complexities of state benefits.

For further information please ring 0181-679 8000.

Your Taxes and Savings

Sally West and the Money Management Council

The definitive annual guide to financial planning for older people, this popular book: explains the tax system in clear, concise language; describes the range of saving and investment options available; and includes model portfolios to illustrate a range of financial scenarios.

For further information please ring 0181-679 8000

Using Your Home as Capital

Cecil Hinton

This best-selling book for home-owners, which is updated annually, gives a detailed explanation of how to capitalise on the value of your home and obtain a regular additional income.

For further information please ring 0181-679 8000

GENERAL

A Buyer's Guide to Retirement Housing

Co-published with the National Housing and Town Planning Council

This book is designed to answer many of the questions older people may have when looking to buy a flat or bungalow in a sheltered scheme. Written in clear and straightforward language, it provides comprehensive information for older people, their families and friends, including topics such as: the design and management of schemes; what to look for when comparing units; the pros and cons; and the charges and costs. Detailed advice is also provided on areas such as the running costs, location and terms of ownership. This popular book – now in its 3rd edition – will provide all the information needed to make an informed decision.

£4.95   0–86242–127–6

If you would like to order any of these titles, please write to the address below, enclosing a cheque or money order for the appropriate amount and made payable to Age Concern England. Credit card orders may be made on 0181-679 8000.

Mail Order Unit
Age Concern England
1268 London Road
London SW16 4ER

Information Line

Age Concern produces over 40 comprehensive factsheets designed to answer many of the questions older people – or those advising them – may have, on topics such as:

- finding and paying for residential and nursing home care
- money benefits
- finding help at home
- legal affairs
- making a Will
- help with heating
- raising income from your home
- transfer of assets

Age Concern offers a factsheet subscription service that presents all the factsheets in a folder, together with regular updates throughout the year. The first year's subscription currently costs £50; an annual renewal thereafter is £25.

To order your FREE factsheet list, phone 0800 00 99 66 (a free call) or write to:

Age Concern
FREEPOST (SWB 30375)
Ashburton
Devon TQ13 7ZZ

Index